A Sense of P. � ᴏok 1

A Sense of Place

Book 1 Place and Space in Britain

Rex Beddis

Oxford University Press 1981

Oxford University Press, Walton Street, Oxford OX2 6DP

London Glasgow New York Toronto
Delhi Bombay Calcutta Madras Karachi
Kuala Lumpur Singapore Hong Kong Tokyo
Nairobi Dar es Salaam Cape Town Salisbury
Melbourne Wellington

and associate companies in
Beirut Berlin Ibadan Mexico City

© Oxford University Press 1981
First published 1981

ISBN 0 19 833433 8

Typeset by Tradespools Limited, Frome, Somerset
Printed in Hong Kong

Preface

This series of three books attempts to bring together elements of descriptive geography, theoretical geography and the more recent 'humanistic' geography that seem appropriate for young people of average ability in the first three years of secondary school. The books provide a carefully structured course complete in itself but also providing a sound basis for pupils who might follow a formal geography course leading to some form of 16+ examination.

The approach of each book is to present a number of ideas through a range of data – text, photographs, drawings, diagrams, statistics, maps and so on. The emphasis is on the understanding of ideas rather than the memorisation of facts, although the acquisition of knowledge of places and peoples is regarded as an important aim. At the same time a wide range of skills should be developed while the themes encourage a clarification of attitudes and values. Pupils are encouraged not only to make judgements from evidence, but also to express their feelings and values however acquired.

Book 1 focusses on basic ideas about location, pattern and process with illustrations from Britain and the experience of British people. Book 2 is concerned with the relationships between environments, resources and people at scales ranging from local to global. In Book 3 the emphasis changes again to economic, social and political aspects of 'development', and to the nature and behaviour of nations and groups. In all three books the aim is to help pupils look at the future as well as understand the present.

The series has been written in the belief that geography can be of real interest and enjoyment to these pupils, and can contribute considerably to their wider education within the school curriculum.

Contents

On the move

A look at the past

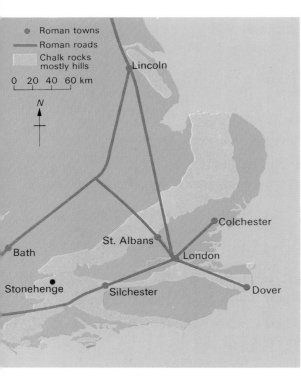

The positions of Stonehenge, London and important Roman towns. Note the areas of chalk and limestone. On this high ground the earliest tracks and roads were formed.

Right: Stonehenge. Why was it built here? *Below*: A disused coal mine in Durham. Why was it dug here?

Scattered around Britain are a number of stone circles built about 4 000 years ago. Stonehenge is one of these. Why was it built? How were the stones taken there and put up in this way? Why is it in this pattern and in this particular place? Only the people who decided to put up the stones, or others who lived at the time, know the answers. We can only guess.

From a few clues left behind it seems that the builders of Stonehenge used tools and weapons of stone and bronze (a mixture of copper and tin). With very simple equipment they cut these massive stones out of the ground and hauled them to this spot. The big sandstone blocks in the inner ring were somehow dragged or carried about 30 kilometres, but the blueish stones from the outer circle must have come from over 300 kilometres away in south-west Wales which is the only place where they are found. Stonehenge must have been important for all this effort to have been made.

The map suggests why the circles were put up in this particular place. Most of Britain at that time was covered with thick, dark forests. The early farmers and cattle herders of southern Britain kept to the treeless, grass-covered chalk hills. We can see that several lines of chalk hills converge and meet in the area where Stonehenge was

built. It would have been a good location for people wanting to gather together for a special event. The circles were probably a sort of temple, and the stones were put up in this pattern so that the sun and stars could be observed at certain times.

About 2 000 years later, Roman armies invaded Britain. The Romans occupied the country for hundreds of years. They built garrison towns for their soldiers, and linked these with long, straight stone roads. This meant their troops could march quickly across the country whatever the weather. One of the small towns and villages scattered around Britain before the Romans arrived was on the banks

of the River Thames, close to where the City of London is now. This was the point nearest to the sea that the river could be forded. The Romans decided that this was a good crossing point for their road linking the south coast ports with the towns of central and northern Britain. The low hills on the north bank gave a dry site above the marshy river banks that were flooded at high tide. So they built a small harbour, a defensive wall around the town on the low hills and a bridge over the river. London began to grow.

London in Roman times

The site of Roman London. The town and bridge were built where the land was least marshy

1 Imagine you were one of the people who decided to build Stonehenge. Write a letter to a friend describing how you intend to build it and why you are going to put it in that particular place.
2 Look at a map of Britain. Describe or draw a map of the route that might have been taken to haul these huge stones from Dyfed in south-west Wales to Stonehenge. What makes people so certain that the stones must have come from this area?
3 What was good about the *site* of London on the north bank of the River Thames? What was good about the *location* of London in this part of Britain for an important Roman town?
4 The mine in the photograph was opened about 100 years ago. Why do you think the mineshaft was dug in this location? How could we try to find out? Why is it likely to be easier to find out about the mine than about Stonehenge?

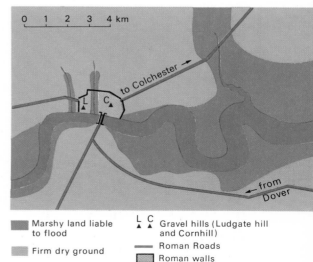

▉ Marshy land liable to flood	L C ▲ ▲	Gravel hills (Ludgate hill and Cornhill)
▉ Firm dry ground	—	Roman Roads
	▭	Roman walls

Where things are

Right: At the junction of the M4 and M5 Motorways in Avon

Two of the thousands of things made in factories and works. A steel oil drilling platform (*above*) and (*below*) a microprocessor

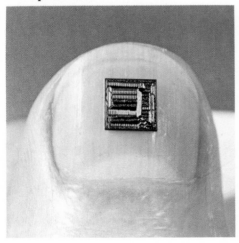

The mine shown on the last page was opened in that particular place because the rocks in the ground beneath it contained coal. It would be foolish to dig a mine if the thing you want doesn't exist there! It was worked for over 100 years, so it must have been a fairly good location. But now it has closed down. Perhaps all the coal has been dug up. Perhaps it can be mined more cheaply elsewhere. Perhaps cheaper or better materials have replaced coal, so the need for it is not as great as it was. Whatever the cause it looks as if this is no longer such a good location for a coal mine.

Thousands of different things are made in factories and workshops of various sorts. Unlike a mine, there are usually many sorts of places where a factory could be built. Some places are good for some sorts of factories, but not very good for others. Some places, such as mountains, are pretty useless for any sort of factory. It would be silly, and very expensive, to make giant oil rigs for use in the North Sea in the middle of Britain, or the centre of a big city. A better sort of place would be on flat, sheltered, unused land near the sea. The north-east coast of Scotland, near the oilfields, would be such a place.

Microchips are very small and cheap to transport. They are beginning to be used in most parts of the country. You could build a microchip or electronics factory in many more places than an oil rig works. But low costs of transport are only one thing that makes a place suitable for a factory. Availability of labour is another. With such things in mind it is a fact that some places are better than others for the location of an electronics factory or any light industry.

Just as there are good and bad locations for a mine or factory, so there are good and bad routes for railways, canals and roads. The shortest and quickest route between two places may not also be the cheapest to build because of the need for bridges and tunnels. It might also cause a lot of nuisance and damage to the places it goes through. In the end a longer route might prove the best and cheapest.

Everyday things in your home and street also have good or bad locations – bus stops, telephone kiosks, pillar boxes, bus routes, shops, clubs, play areas and so on. If all the locations of any one of these is shown on a map – all the pillar boxes, or all the bus routes, for example – a pattern will be seen. This book is going to look at where things are located, and the patterns they make. We shall keep asking the question 'Why is it there?'.

1 If all the coal was dug up, the coal mine would never open again. But if there was still some coal in the ground what would make it worthwhile to open it again?
2 Think of any shop, factory, school or road that has been closed or has changed from one place to another in your area. What was bad about the location for it to close down or move? If it moved somewhere else in your area what do you think was better about the new location?
3 Why might the quickest route between two places be more expensive to build than a longer one? How might a new road or railway cause damage or be a nuisance?
4 What is a good location for a post or pillar box, a telephone kiosk, a bus stop, a parade of shops? How might a location that is 'good' for you or your family, be 'bad' for your friends and their families?
5 On a map of your area mark all the post boxes, shops and bus stops. Use three different colours or symbols and a key. Say for each whether the pattern is clustered, regularly spaced or scattered.

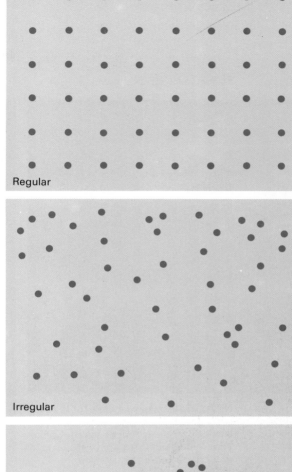

Regular

Irregular

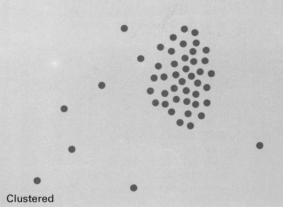

Clustered

Above: The patterns things make. What could these points represent: people on a beach, animals in a field, cars in a car park, or villages in the countryside? Without a key we cannot say. Are the patterns sheer chance, or is there a reason for them?

Left: Why are all these things in these places: it is chance or have they been put there deliberately? Do they seem to be well or badly placed?

11

Rocks, quarries and mines

Fossils in a slab of limestone rock

Right: Millions of years ago these beds of sandstone were once flat layers at the bottom of the sea. Since then they have been folded and lifted above sea level by great earth movements

A limestone quarry in the Mendip Hills, near the famous Cheddar Gorge

The surface or 'crust' of the earth is made of rocks. Very often these rocks are covered with grass and trees, or hidden beneath a layer of soil, mud, sand or pebbles. The underlying rocks can often be seen where the land is too steep for soil or plant cover, or where the sea has formed cliffs, or where a quarry has been dug.

Rocks differ in many ways – in colour, hardness, age, how they were formed and what minerals they are made of. Some have been produced by the cooling and hardening of hot, molten rock called 'magma' that has come from deep in the crust which is 200 km thick. Granite rocks and lava that comes from volcanoes are formed this way. Other rocks have been formed from grains of mud or sand, dead vegetation, shells of sea creatures or other minerals that have settled on the bottoms of lakes and seas. As these layers get thicker and become covered with more deposits they harden into beds of rock. Shale, sandstone, chalk, and limestone are examples. Because they are made of sediments they are called 'sedimentary' rocks.

Some rocks are used for building either directly as stones or changed into bricks or cement. Others are crushed and made into chemicals or fertilizers or used to make roads. Some such as coal can be burned and used as a fuel. Yet others contain metals. Rocks which contain metals are called ores – iron ore is a good example.

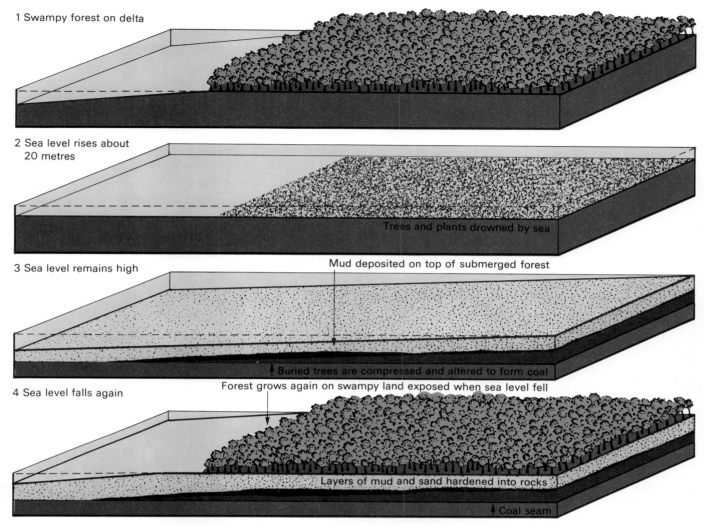

1 Swampy forest on delta

2 Sea level rises about 20 metres

Trees and plants drowned by sea

3 Sea level remains high

Mud deposited on top of submerged forest

Buried trees are compressed and altered to form coal

4 Sea level falls again

Forest grows again on swampy land exposed when sea level fell

Layers of mud and sand hardened into rocks

Coal seam

Many of these rocks are dug out of the crust in open quarries or pits. If the valuable rocks are deep below the surface they have to be reached by drilling shafts down through the overlying rock. You will only find quarries and deep mines where these rocks, minerals and ores are. Even when valuable rocks are known to exist in a place they may still not be quarried or mined – it may be too expensive or too difficult. People sometimes object to quarries and mines being dug because they scar the landscape and use valuable land.

1 Draw a line 6 cm long. Label to say 'Distance from the surface to the centre of the earth'. Now mark off 2 mm from one end. Label to say 'Thickness of earth's crust'.
2 Look at the buildings shown in this book, or think of those you see around your home and school. Describe how rocks or their products have been used in some of these buildings.
3 What are the following rocks used for? – coal, granite, clay, chalk, iron ore.
4 Imagine you are standing on the edge of the limestone quarry. Describe the scene – what you can see, feel and hear.
5 Valuable ores and minerals from the earth's crust are called 'non-renewable' resources! What do you think it means?

How coal is formed

Giant machines used in mining iron ore. The cover of unwanted rock is removed and the ore then scooped up and loaded into railway trucks

Old and new mines

An old colliery pit head and miners' cottages

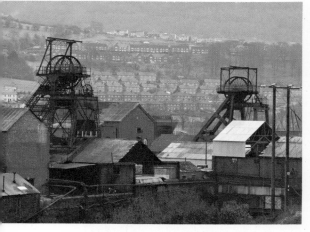

Right: Kellingley colliery, Yorkshire. A new mine

Miner operating a trepanner – a coal cutter

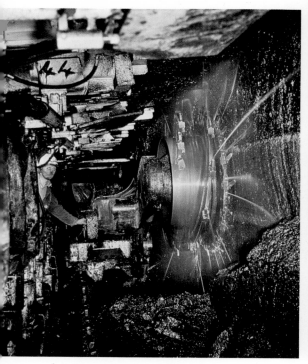

Coal is a sedimentary rock. The way it is formed was described on page 13. The coal found in Britain was deposited millions of years ago. Since then most of the beds have been tilted or folded, so in some places they are at or near the surface while in others they are deep underground.

The earliest mines were where the coal seams lay on or near the surface. These places are known as the 'exposed' part of the coalfield. The coal was fairly easy to mine. The collieries were small and the shafts not very deep. Most of the digging and loading of coal was done by hand. It was a dark, dirty and dangerous job. The miners and their families lived in rows of small houses near the colliery or 'pit'. A huge mound of rock waste dug up with the coal towered over the pit village. These 'spoil heaps' or 'slag heaps' of grey stone and rubble usually smouldered and smelled and were often dangerous when perched on the sides of valleys. Sometimes they collapsed on to the village below,

killing many people. Most of these old mines have been closed down either because most of the coal has been dug up, or because they were too small and became too costly to run.

Modern mines are bigger and usually have deeper shafts to reach the seams of coal in the 'concealed' part of the coalfield. Some of the mines being planned and prepared for the next ten years are in the open countryside. New towns will have to be built or miners taken to work from their present homes by bus.

A great deal of machinery is used in a modern mine. In the photograph we can see a miner operating a trepanner – a revolving wheel with sharp cutting teeth that bites into the seam of coal. The cut coal is loaded automatically on to conveyor belts and taken by electric or diesel-hauled underground train to the cages at the bottom of the shafts. Other miners will be moving the steel roof supports and shifting the conveyor belts as the trepanner cuts into the coalface. Yet others will be filling in the space behind the supports with fallen rock, operating the trains and checking the power and ventilation. On the surface men will be screening and washing the coal, sorting it into different sizes, operating engines and doing all sorts of office work. A modern mine is a busy place with work going on day and night.

1 Copy the diagram. Put the labels 'Old mine on exposed coalfield' and 'New mine on concealed coalfield' in the correct places.
2 Imagine you are the coalminer working the trepanner. Describe what the work is like and how you feel about it.
3 Compare the scene of the old and the new mines and their surroundings. What clues are there that Kellingley is a fairly new mine?
4 The letters A; B; C; D; on the map refer to coalfields in Scotland; South Wales; Northumberland and Durham; and Yorkshire-Nottinghamshire-Derbyshire. Which letters stand for which coalfield? Look at the bar graph and say which is the most important of the coalfields.
5 Look at the table. What was the change over 20 years in a) number of collieries, b) the number of miners, c) the percentage (%) of coal dug out by machines, d) the amount of coal mined?.
6 Look at the bar graph. What are the main uses of coal?

Exposed and concealed parts of a coalfield. When the coal-bearing rocks are tilted then some of the coalfield will be 'exposed' and some hidden or 'concealed' beneath newer rocks

Changes in coalmining between 1955 and 1975

	1955	1975
Output (deep-mined) in million tonnes	211	117
Active collieries	850	246
Manpower (thousands)	699	246
Mechanised output (%)	11.1	93.5

The main coalfields of Britain

Coalfields

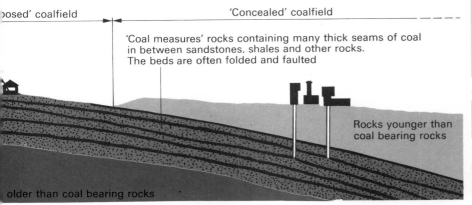

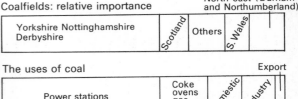

Coalfields: relative importance				North-east (Durham and Northumberland)
Yorkshire Nottinghamshire Derbyshire	Scotland	Others	S. Wales	

The uses of coal				Export
Power stations	Coke ovens gas	Domestic	Industry	

'Exposed' coalfield · 'Concealed' coalfield

'Coal measures' rocks containing many thick seams of coal in between sandstones, shales and other rocks. The beds are often folded and faulted

Rocks younger than coal bearing rocks

older than coal bearing rocks

Power from water

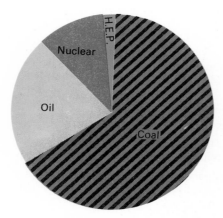

Types of electricity power station in Britain. The size of each slice shows how much electricity out of the total is made in that sort of power station

Men have always used simple machines involving levers and pulleys to do their work. For thousands of years they have also used the power of wind and running water to drive their machines.

The earliest mills and factories, where machines were put together in one big building, were for making cloth from wool and cotton, for grinding and forging iron and steel and for milling flour. The machines in these mills and factories were driven by wheels and belts fixed to a water wheel. The wheel was turned by the flow of water in a stream or river. This is why the earliest factories and mills were in steepsided valleys with swift-flowing streams, or on the banks of big rivers. Suitable areas in England were in the valleys of the Cotswold hills in Gloucestershire and the Pennine hills in Yorkshire and Lancashire.

At a later date the coal-burning steam engine was invented. In many ways the steam engine was better than the water wheel, and it began to replace the wheel as a source of power. New factories were built near coalfields.

Later on new ways of making and using electricity were discovered. The diagram shows how flowing water can be transported to turn the turbine blades to make electricity in a power station. Because water is used in this type of power station, it is called a hydro-electric power station (HEP).

A disused water wheel

Right: The blade of a turbine. Compare it with the disused water wheel above

16

Left: The site for an underground power station being blasted out of the Welsh Hills

The Dinarwi power station in the Welsh mountains. During the day electricity is made as water flows from the upper to the lower reservoir. At night the station pumps water back to the the upper reservoir

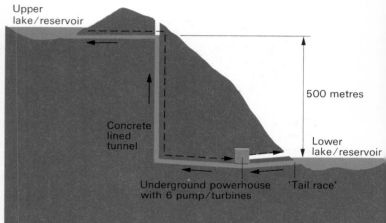

The best place for an HEP station is where there are powerfully flowing rivers that never dry up. Since there are not many places like this the flow of water has to be man-made. This is done by trapping a mass of water in a lake behind a reservoir wall or dam, and leading the water down through steel pipes into the power station. Most of these reservoirs and power stations in Britain are in the hillier regions. This is where it is easiest to build the reservoirs and where rainfall is heaviest. Sometimes the pipes and tunnels carrying the water from the reservoir to the turbines cut dozens of kilometres through the mountains.

The HEP stations in Britain are not big by world standards. Some people think that more electricity could be made in Britain by using the rise and fall of the tides around our coasts. The most likely site is the Severn Estuary. If a tidal power station is built there it will be the biggest in the world.

1   What are some of the disadvantages of using **a**) wind, **b**) water flowing in a stream or river, to drive machinery?
2   Put into words 'How electricity is made in an HEP station'.
3   Where would you expect most HEP stations in Britain to be? Using a relief map of the British Isles from your atlas, give two reasons for your choice.
4   Copy the diagram showing 'Types of electricity power station in Britain'. Colour in the proportion of power produced by HEP stations only. Give your diagram a new title.

Where the Severn Barrage and tidal power station might be

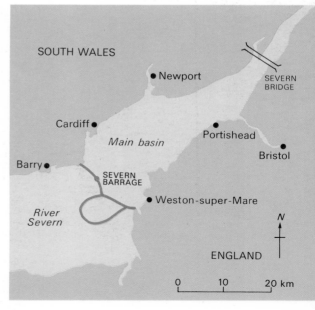

17

Power stations

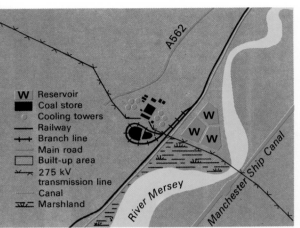

W	Reservoir
■	Coal store
⊙	Cooling towers
——	Railway
╂╂	Branch line
⋯⋯	Main road
▭	Built-up area
╳╳	275 kV transmission line
──	Canal
⚒	Marshland

A map (*above*) and photograph (*below*) of a modern coal-fired power station at Fiddler's Ferry on the River Mersey

The turbines that make electricity can be driven by steam as well as flowing water. If water is heated to boiling point and above, steam is produced. Jets of steam can be used to turn the turbine blades just as the jets of water do. Because heat is used to produce the steam, these are called 'thermal' power stations.

Different sorts of fuel can be used to heat the water. Coal, gas or oil can be burnt – just as in a hot water system in a house. Unlike the heating system in a house, though, a big power station can also be fuelled by heat from a nuclear reaction.

A thermal power station needs large amounts of water for cooling. This is because the steam which is produced by the heat from the furnaces needs to be turned back into water to be used again. (The word for this is 'condensed'.) One of the most striking parts of a thermal station is the collection of cooling towers with steam rising out of them. Thermal power stations need to be near a source of cooling water. That is why they are so often located along the banks of a big river or at the coast.

Power stations that burn coal or oil are best located near coal fields, oil refineries or oil terminals. They may also be found near ports where these heavy and bulky fuels can be unloaded from boats. Coal-fired stations are sometimes fed with coal delivered by barges, but nowadays many use a 'merry-go-round' railway system. The coal trains go backwards and forwards between mine and power station and are loaded and unloaded without stopping.

How a thermal power station works

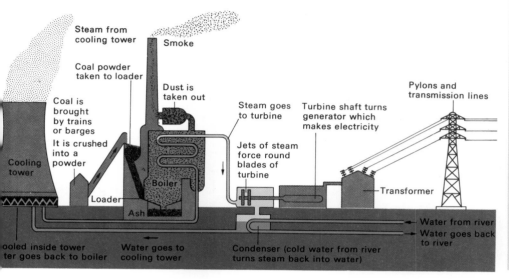

Above: Nuclear power stations in Britain

Nuclear power stations use small amounts of uranium as fuel for their reactors. They could therefore be located wherever there was a good supply of cooling water and flat land capable of supporting the massive buildings. But there is always a danger of a leak of radioactive material, or of an explosion. So nuclear stations are usually built away from large towns and cities.

1   Draw a picture or a map of the power station at Fiddler's Ferry and label to show the cooling towers, the station and its furnace chimney, the stockyards where the coal is stored and the source of cooling water.

2   Imagine you are writing a letter to a friend describing what you had seen on a recent visit to Fiddler's Ferry Power Station. What would you say about the scene of the barges and the power station?

3   What do you think are three good things about the site and location of the nuclear power station at Wylfa? From the map say where it is.

4   What kind of location do all the nuclear power stations (except the one in North Wales) share in common? Why is this?

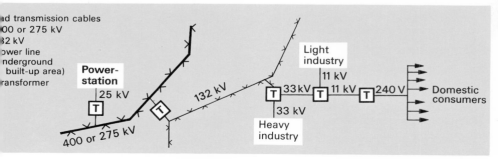

Wylfa nuclear power station. Can you give one reason for its location in an isolated spot by the sea?

Left: The electricity grid system. The electricity is carried from the station at high voltage along cables carried on pylons. The voltage is reduced for use in factories and in the home

19

Making iron and steel

How a blast furnace works

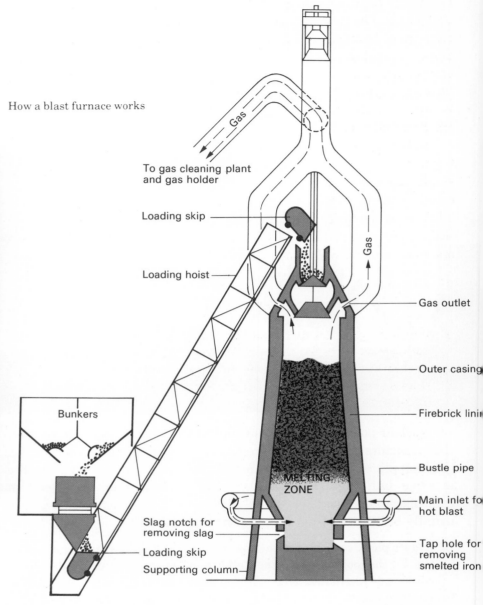

Ironbridge: the first ever cast iron bridge. It crosses the River Severn close to the town of Coalbrookdale where iron was first smelted with charcoal

Pouring molten steel from a converter into containers

Iron is made by heating or 'smelting' iron ore in a furnace. In early days this was done by mixing the ore with glowing charcoal. The charcoal had been made by burning timber from trees in a special way. As you might expect these early furnaces were found where there was a good and easily mined supply of iron ore and where there were forests nearby to provide the timber for making into charcoal.

Then a much better way of smelting iron ore on a large scale was discovered. This was by heating the ore with coke made from coal, and adding limestone to the furnace to make the smelting more efficient. Some of the first coke-burning iron furnaces were at Coalbrookdale on the banks of the River Severn in Shropshire. The first-ever cast iron bridge at nearby Ironbridge is a beautiful reminder of the skill of the ironworkers. Iron works were built all over the country, but the greatest concentrations were near the coalmines. South Wales and the area around Sheffield became iron- and steel-making centres.

The iron was shaped either by pouring the hot molten metal into moulds made in sand or by beating the white-hot metal with hammers and forges. The next important discovery was how to make steel from iron. Steel is much stronger and has more uses than iron. This was done by burning out some impurities from the molten iron and adding carefully measured amounts of other chemicals. This is now done by blowing oxygen through the molten iron in a large steel container known as a Basic Oxygen Converter. Scrap steel can also be re-smelted and used again.

Molten steel is poured from the converters into containers and taken by rail to the steel rolling mills nearby. Here all sorts of steel shapes are made – slabs, sheets, coils of wire, girders, thin plate to be coated with tin, pipes and so on. These products are then taken to steel-using factories all over the country. Steelmaking is a very skilled job, and nowadays a lot of the work is done by automated machines controlled by computers.

Forging steel

1 Make a list of ten things that you can think of that are made of iron or steel. There are many examples given in this book if you cannot think of any.
2 Why is it a good idea for an iron works to be built either near a supply of coking coal or a supply of iron ore? Where would be a good place to build a steelworks if iron ore from other countries had to be used?
3 Draw a simple diagram to show the stages by which iron ore is turned into steel slabs or girders.
4 Imagine you are in charge of pouring the molten steel into steel moulds or containers. Describe your thoughts and feelings about what you see.

Rolling steel. The man in the foreground is controlling the rollers that shape the steel

An integrated steelworks

Port Talbot steelworks and the nearby town in the early evening

The cheapest way to make large amounts of steel is in one very big works where the blast furnaces, converters and rolling mills are close together. These giant works, costing millions of pounds to build, are known as 'integrated' iron and steel works.

Over two-thirds of the iron ore used in British steelworks these days comes from foreign orefields. The ore is carried in giant ships to cut down the cost of transporting this bulky and heavy raw material. Cost of transport is also the reason why most of the new integrated works are built on the coast. Scunthorpe is an exception, but there the steelworks is linked to its iron-ore port at Immingham by a special railway.

Older steelworks such as those found in Sheffield are mixed among houses and steel-using factories. The most modern ones cover vast areas of land and are outside the nearby towns. Thousands of workers travel to and from work by bus or car. Most of the older iron and steel works have been closed down. They were either too small, badly placed to receive raw materials and fuel, or had old-fashioned furnaces. It was impossible for them to make large amounts of steel as cheaply as the big new integrated works. On the other hand the skills learned by the steelworkers are valuable. So works making small amounts of special steels still survive in places like Sheffield – even though they may not be in the ideal place.

A huge ore carrier being unloaded at Port Talbot

The boarded-up houses are a sign of the end of Corby as a steelmaking town. July 1979

Steelmaking areas in Britain

In the late 1970s even more modern works were closed down. Too much steel was being made. But it was also being made inefficiently. The managers of British Steel – the nationalised company that runs most of our steelworks – said that inland works such as those at Ebbw Vale, Shotton and Corby would have to stop making steel. The local workers and managers often disagreed and tried to stop the closures. The effect of closing the steelworks was very hard on the local towns. Corby, for example, had been built as a steel workers' town in the 1930s, and many people came from Scotland and elsewhere to work and live there. A modern steelworks employs a lot of people, and if it closes down there is a lot of unemployment and many families and shopkeepers suffer.

1 Describe the location of the Redcar integrated steelworks within Britain, the site of the steelworks and the approximate area of land covered by the plant. What are some of the attractions of the site for a modern integrated steelworks?
2 Draw a simple diagram to show the following facts about where the iron ore used in British steelworks comes from: British ore 9 million tonnes. Foreign ore 22 million tonnes. Total ore used 31 million tonnes.
3 Name the big integrated steel works shown on the map – they are given in the key
4 Give one reason for and one reason against closing a big steelworks like the one at Corby.

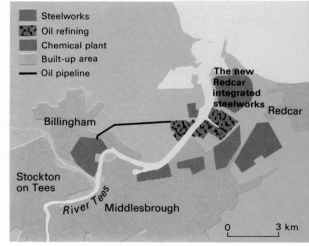

The location of the integrated steel works at Redcar

Light industry

Some manufacturing industries, such as steelmaking or shipbuilding, either use a lot of materials or use very bulky materials. These industries need to be in certain places to cut down on the cost of transporting raw materials and products to and from the factories and works. These are sometimes called 'heavy' industries.

Other industries have much lighter and more easily carried raw materials and products. In many cases the things they make are wanted all over the country, so there is no need for these factories to be near a particular 'market' either. The factory *could* be in many possible places (as long as it is near fairly large numbers of people). What makes the owners or managers of a company choose to put their factory in one place rather than another? This question can be asked about factories making things as different as motor cars, clothing, biscuits or drinks. Some of the answers are given in this advertisement.

1   What five reasons are given in the advertisement for attracting the Cinzano factory to Telford?
2   What messages do the pictures in the advertisement tell us about the place? What have they got to do with attracting a factory to the area?
3   What does the map in the advertisement tell us about Telford. Compare it with the other map. What are the differences between them?
4   What are the main differences between these factories and the steelworks described on page 22? Think about site, shape and size.

Telford New Town

Factories designed for light industry at Telford in Shropshire

Factory ship

Right: A trawler hauling in the catch from the stern

A huge Russian factory ship

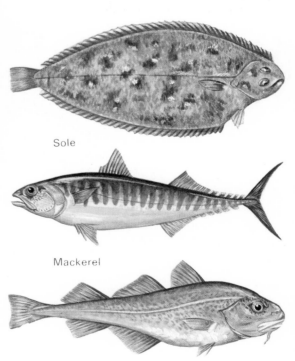

Sole

Mackerel

Cod

The main types of fish caught by the Falmouth trawlers

Factories are places where raw materials are processed into some other more valuable product, such as wheat into flour and flour into bread. Usually factories are on land, but there is no reason why they cannot be on board a ship at sea. The large ships in the photograph are floating factories. They receive their raw materials – mackerel – from the catcher-trawlers that fish where the shoals gather at certain times of the year. The factory ships then fillet and freeze, can or salt the catch or turn the fish into fertilizer or animal food. Some of the larger trawlers can also freeze fish and are called freezer-trawlers.

Like herring, but unlike cod and 'white' fish, mackerel are surface swimmers. They appear in large numbers off the coast of Scotland in summer and autumn, and a little later off the coast of Cornwall in autumn and winter.

Most of the factory ships off the British coast are foreign. Because foreign ships are not allowed to fish within a certain distance of the coast (to prevent over-fishing) the trawlers that supply these factory ships are British. In October they come from ports all around the country to Falmouth to trawl for mackerel. About 90 per cent of their catch is loaded on to foreign freezer-trawlers from such countries as Russia, Poland, Bulgaria and East Germany. The British ships trawl during the week and then put in to Falmouth or Penzance harbours to take on fuel and water. Many of the crews fly to their home ports for the week-end. The bigger foreign vessels stay in the area until March or April when they sail back to Eastern Europe.

In this example the raw material for the factory is not in a fixed place like iron ore, but moves from place to place. The factory moves to the location of the raw materials – for the few months that they are there. It manufactures its products, stores them and then moves off to sell its goods back in its own country.

We have seen that some resources can be used up – all the coal or iron ore can be dug out of a mine. In the same way, unless care is taken the mackerel will be used up by over-fishing as the herring was in the 1970s. The British fishing industry is certainly a declining one at the moment. This is partly because there are fewer fish and partly because foreign-caught fish can be sold more cheaply than British-caught fish.

1 There are many different ways of preparing fish for sale. Name some of the ways fish are prepared for sale in British supermarkets and fishmongers.

2 Draw pictures of the three types of ships in Falmouth harbour in order of size and then add the following labels to them; **a**) catching fleet – small ships about 200 tons **b**) freezer trawlers – about 2 000 tons **c**) factory ships – about 20 000 tons.

3 British ships have been stopped from fishing for herring around the coast of Britain. Why do you think this is so? Why have they also been stopped from fishing for cod within 200 miles of the coast of Iceland? Do you think Iceland is right or wrong?

4 Why are the waters off the coast of Cornwall a good location for foreign factory ships from October to March, but not for the rest of the year?

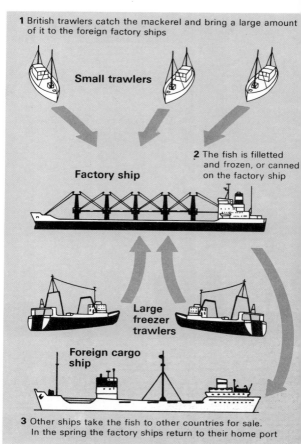

1 British trawlers catch the mackerel and bring a large amount of it to the foreign factory ships

Small trawlers

2 The fish is filletted and frozen, or canned on the factory ship

Factory ship

Large freezer trawlers

Foreign cargo ship

3 Other ships take the fish to other countries for sale. In the spring the factory ships return to their home port

Diagram showing how about 150 British trawlers feed 25–30 freezer vessels and about five factory ships

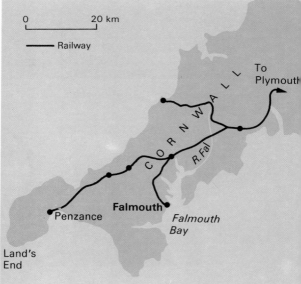

The location of Falmouth

Left: The arrival of factory ships and freezer vessels near Falmouth for the mackerel season

27

Cereals

Ploughing the land in autumn before the winter frosts and snow

Smoothing out the soil in spring before planting

The machines opposite are harvesting a crop of wheat on a hot sunny day in August. The one on the right is moving away from us cutting the wheat as it goes. Inside the machine the grain is separated from the stalk or straw. This is known as 'threshing'. The straw is then left behind the harvester in a long trail on the ground. Later on, other machines will scoop this up and pack it into bales to be taken to the farm buildings. When the harvester is full of grain, a lorry or tractor and trailer will pull alongside. The long arm will swing over the trailer and the grain will be emptied into it. We can see this happening with the harvester in the distance. All this is happening on an arable farm, which is a farm where only crops are grown.

Wheat, barley and oats are the main cereal crops grown in Britain. The grain is used for feeding people or as fodder for animals to eat. Many foods we eat come from plants. The farmers job is to help these plants grow as well and as quickly as possible – to produce high yields. Different plants need different conditions to grow well. Temperatures have to be above a certain point for a long enough period for the plant to grow. If frosts or low temperatures happen during this time the plant may die. Soils need to be deep enough to take the plant roots. They also need to be well drained so that air and water can get to the plant roots. The farmer prepares the soil by ploughing – turning it over – and harrowing – breaking it up into smaller crumbs before drilling or planting the crop.

The plants take in food from the soil through their roots. If the soil is not rich enough the farmer adds fertilizer. Plant food cannot be taken out of the soil year after year without some being put back. Some food can be put back if a different crop is grown – if a field is planted with sugar beet after cereals, for example. The food is taken in dissolved in water through the roots, so it is important for plants to

The cereal farmer's year

Cereals	Jan.	Feb.	March	April	May	June	July	August	Sept.	Oct.	Nov.	Dec.
Autumn sown wheat, barley	Crops growing slowly during winter			Fertilizer added / rolling	Spraying with weed killer			Harvesting	Straw baled and stacked	Ploughing, cultivating, sowing/drilling →		
Spring sown mostly barley, some wheat												

Combine harvesters at work in big hedgeless fields. Because of the cost of these machines some farmers hire them or pay other people to harvest their crop for them

be well watered. If there is not enough rain, then the farmer may need to irrigate his crops to get good yields. Another problem is that weeds may choke the growing crop, or the plants be attacked by disease or insects. The farmer usually applies weed-killer and pesticides to protect the crop. Sun is needed for ripening, and this is something over which the farmer has least control!

If he has chosen a suitable place, prepared the soil properly, carefully tended the plants (and had reasonable luck with the weather!) then the farmer should get a good crop.

1. Describe the fields being used for crop growing in the photograph. What do you notice about their size? Is the relief flat and gentle or steep and rugged? What is there about the fields that allows machines to be used? What sort of land would not be suitable?

2. Copy the diagram of the farmers year, but instead of showing 'winter' wheat show the main events of growing 'spring' wheat. These are **a**) Ploughing – November to February **b**) Cultivation, adding fertilizer and drilling the seed – March and April **c**) Harvesting – mid-August and September

3. Some crops are sold to markets and greengrocers, others to factories to be processed or made into something else before being sold. What are some of the things that happen to wheat, barley, sugar beet, potatoes, peas?

4. Where are the main cereal growing areas in Britain? Look at the map on page 31 and try and say why they are in these places.

Wheat (*above*) and barley (*below*)

Root crops, fruit and vegetables

Harvesting Dwarf French beans for the frozen food market

A fruit farm in Kent

Sugar beet being delivered to factories for refining into sugar

Some farmers keep animals as well as grow crops and this is often known as mixed farming. Many crops besides cereals are grown on arable and mixed farms. Such crops include potatoes, sugar beet, beans, peas and cabbage.

The farmer often plants different crops in a field from year to year – wheat or barley followed by sugar beet or potatoes or beans and then perhaps grass. This is because each crop takes different foods from the soil, and some add things to the soil that other crops need. This 'rotation of crops' helps keep the soil rich. If he wants to grow only one crop then he will need to add lots of fertilizer or animal manure to the soil or the yields will fall.

Sometimes the farmer will sell his crops direct to merchants or to big markets. But nowadays many are under contract to sell to sugar beet factories, flour mills or freezing and canning firms such as Birds Eye. They arrange to sell all their crop to these firms before they are harvested, rather than taking them to be bought for whatever price they can get at a local market. The sugar beet factories start to make the beet into sugar in October, when vast amounts of beet are carried by lorry to the factory and the pulp left after refining is taken back to the farms for animal food.

Crops, such as fresh vegetables like tomatoes and lettuce which need a lot of attention and fetch a high price, are grown on special farms called market gardens. They are often grown in glasshouses or greenhouses where the air temperature, the amount of moisture in the air (the humidity) and the amount of water and food in the soil can all be carefully controlled. Although this costs a lot, it is worth the expense. Market gardens and greenhouse areas are often quite close to towns and cities. Another type of farm specialises in producing tree fruits such as apples, pears and plums or bush fruits like blackberries and raspberries and strawberries. It is common these days to see road-side stalls selling fresh fruit and vegetables, or signs inviting you to 'pick your own crops'. The result of this specialisation is that a far greater variety of fruit and vegetables is seen in shops nowadays than twenty years ago. Such crops as sweet corn, red and green peppers, aubergines and courgettes are now quite common. Many homes nowadays have freezers and housewives are encouraged to buy such 'exotic' crops in season when the price is low and freeze them for eating later.

The sort of crops a farmer grows is influenced by the environment – the shape of the land, the soil and the weather – but also by the price he can get from the factory, market or customer.

The variety of food available at one British greengrocer's shop

1 What crops are imported into Britain because they cannot be grown here? What crops are imported because our farmers do not grow enough or because they are cheaper to buy overseas?
2 Why is it sensible for fresh vegetables and fruit to be grown fairly close to towns and cities? Why are some people prepared to pay more for fresh food than for the same things frozen or canned?
3 Name a few big food companies – what are their products? How do they advertise their products in magazines, newspapers and on TV?
4 What two things does the graph tell us about changes in British farming?

The most important farming areas

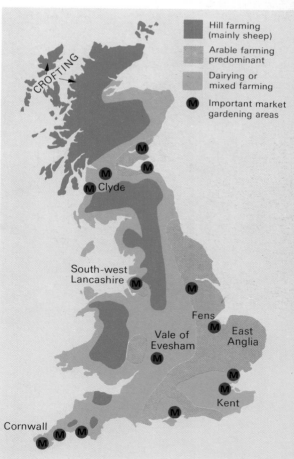

Hill farming (mainly sheep)
Arable farming predominant
Dairying or mixed farming
Ⓜ Important market gardening areas

Changes in British farming

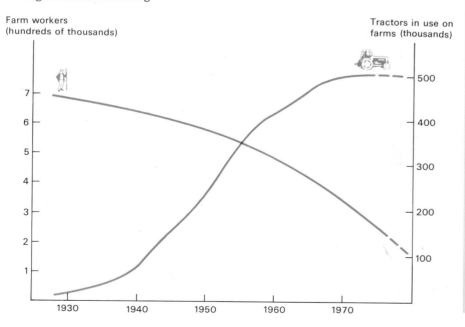

Milk and meat

One of the most important types of farming in Britain is dairying. A dairy farm is one where only dairy cattle are kept. Some dairy cattle are also kept on mixed farms. Three million or so dairy cows provide us with milk and milk products such as cheese, butter, cream and yoghurt.

The average size of a herd on a modern dairy farm is about 50 cows. This is just about the number that can be carefully looked after by one cowman. Cows that have given birth to calves will produce milk for about eight months afterwards. They have to be milked twice a day, seven days a week. The milking parlour is part of the main farm buildings. The cows are brought in from the fields and led into stalls. They are fed a carefully balanced mixture of barley or other grain and a special cattle food called 'cake'. At the same time they are milked by electric milking machine. The milk given by each cow is measured and automatically pumped to the cooler. At regular intervals it is collected by a milk tanker and taken to the local dairy.

A Hereford bull with Friesian heifers

Right, below: Cows being milked by machine

Below: Cattle grazing on pasture

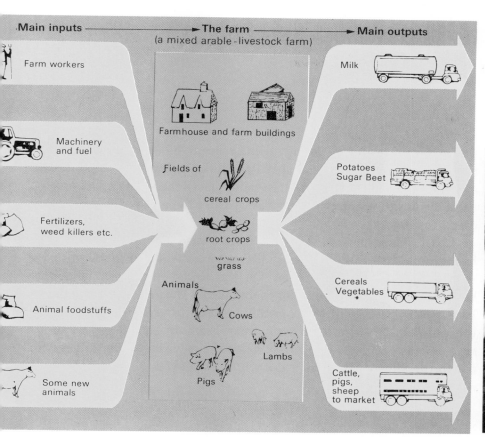

Main inputs ──────→ The farm ──────→ Main outputs
(a mixed arable-livestock farm)

Farm workers

Machinery and fuel

Fertilizers, weed killers etc.

Animal foodstuffs

Some new animals

Farmhouse and farm buildings

Fields of

cereal crops

root crops

grass

Animals

Cows

Pigs

Lambs

Milk

Potatoes
Sugar Beet

Cereals
Vegetables

Cattle, pigs, sheep to market

Left: Inputs and outputs in a mixed farm

An intensive pig fattening unit

Farm buildings in Sussex. Do you think that this is a prosperous farm?

Many of the fields will be in grass, either as permanent pasture on wetter land or sown grass as part of a rotation of crops. Some will be grazed by the cows while the rest will be cut for hay or silage. Other fields will be used for growing crops such as oats, barley or kale for fodder or wheat, barley, roots and vegetables for sale.

The dairy farmer gets his income from the sale of milk to the Milk Marketing Board and the sale of the male calves for fattening up as veal or beef. He keeps some of the female calves (called heifers) to add to his own herd and sells the others to other dairy herds.

The best conditions for dairying and fattening cattle are in places with mild winters with little frost or snow, and where there is a moderate rainfall throughout the year. In these conditions the grass should grow well if cared for. It also helps if the land is not too hilly. There are a few areas where dairying is very important – Somerset, South Wales, Cheshire and the lowlands of Scotland for example. Fattening cattle for beef is important in the rich farmlands of the Midlands and in eastern Scotland.

1 Jerseys and Ayreshires are important dairy cattle breeds. An important beef cattle breed is the Hereford. Where are these places?
2 Look at the butter and other dairy produce in your local grocer's shop or supermarket. Name the main brands and the countries they come from.
3 Draw a sketch of the dairy cattle scene, and label to show some of the features that make it good cattle farming country.
4 Many poultry, pigs and some cattle are nowadays raised in intensive farm units – sometimes called 'factory farming'. What does this mean? What are the arguments for and against factory farming?

Hill sheep farm

A ewe and her newly born lamb

Sheep farms are often found in hilly areas of Britain such as the mountains and hills of Central Wales, the Lake District, the Pennines and the Highlands of Scotland. In these places the slopes are too steep, the soils too thin and poor and the weather too severe for large-scale crop growing.

Local stones are used for the farm house and buildings. In the background are the hills and 'fells' where the sheep graze on open moorland during the summer. On the lower slopes the fields are bounded by stone walls or hedges and trees. Most of the fields always have grass growing in them. Some are used to grow fodder crops for the animals or sown with temporary grass in rotation with other crops. Some of the grass in these fields is cut for hay or for silage and fed to the sheep. Silage is grass which is packed in a large airtight container called a 'silo'.

Sheep in the snow. Feeding sheep can be a big problem in harsh winters

Right: A hill sheep farm in the Lake District

Some of the breeds of British hill sheep are Blackface, Welsh, Herdwick and Swaledale. They all have to be tough to survive the harsh winters and heavy snow that can fall in the mountains. They also all have to be able to walk long distances over the steep hillsides looking for grazing land.

The sheep are brought down from the hills during the winter and kept near the farm buildings until lambing. Mating takes place in November, and the lambs are born the following spring in April. The ewes and their lambs are then taken into the hills for the summer. With the help of his sheepdogs the farmer brings them in for dipping against insects and pests in June or July. He brings them in again for the market sales in the nearby town in the autumn. Here they may be sold to lowland farmers for fattening up for sale as lamb. The main income from the hill farm is from the sale of wool and lambs.

The farm buildings are small and fairly simple. There is no need for expensive machinery, fertilizers or seed. Few people are needed to run the farm, but dogs are essential! Costs are low, but so are profits. Many young people find the life hard and lonely, and there are fewer hill farms now than there used to be.

Shearing sheep

1 What are some of the differences between the relief of the land and the weather in these areas of hill sheep farming and those of arable farming in eastern England as shown in the photographs on page 29?
2 List all the features in the photograph of the hill farm that are mentioned in the description.
3 Draw a diagram of the sheep farmer's year similar to that on page 28.
4 What are the names of the hill and mountain areas shown on the map on page 31?
5 What do you think you would like and dislike about being the son or daughter of a hill sheep farmer?

Sheep auction

Land use, hill slope, soil and drainage

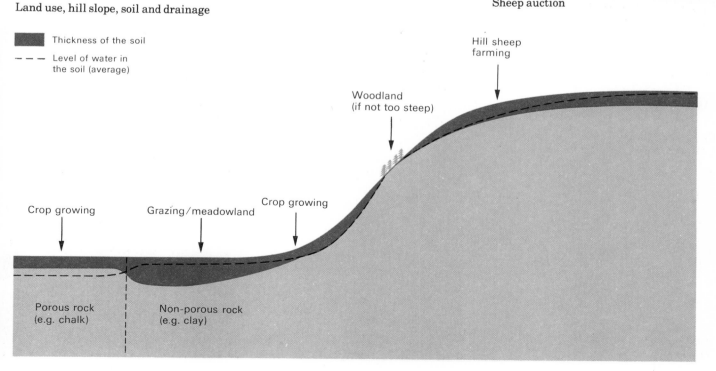

Thickness of the soil

– – – Level of water in the soil (average)

Hill sheep farming

Woodland (if not too steep)

Crop growing

Crop growing

Grazing/meadowland

Crop growing

Porous rock (e.g. chalk)

Non-porous rock (e.g. clay)

Mountains and hill country

Walkers on the Pennine Way in the Peak District in Derbyshire

Right, below: Ice-carved hillslopes and steep edges in the Brecon Beacons. The peak is 886 metres above sea level

Below: Hill and mountain areas in Britain

British mountains are quite small compared with some mountains in other parts of the world. To those who live in the lowlands, though, they seem very high indeed! It is hard to believe that some of the rocks that make up these mountains were once laid down as sedimentary beds in ancient seas. Great earth movements have buckled and forced them up to these heights. What we see now is what is left after millions of years of wearing down and erosion.

It can be very cold in the mountains, especially at night. Any water from rain or melting snow that has been trapped in cracks in the rock gets frozen. As it freezes it expands and forces chips and slabs of rock to fall from the mountain face. This frost shattering, along with the wind and the rain, wears the sides of the mountain down and keeps the peaks and ridges sharp and steep.

The main shapes in the highest mountains have been caused by glaciers – rivers of ice – in the past. Ice from frozen snow gathered in hollows near the mountain tops. As more ice was added it moved or flowed down the valleys. It took with it rocks that scratched and gouged out deep U-shaped valleys. The climate of Britain is warmer than it was and the glaciers have now gone. But round 'corrie' lakes are often found in the hollows where the ice collected, and deep, narrow 'ribbon' lakes can be found in the valleys. Some of this mountain scenery can be seen in the photographs and map of the Lake District in the second part of this unit.

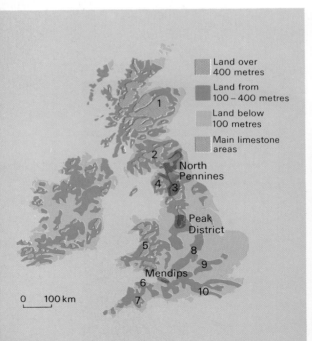

Land over 400 metres

Land from 100 – 400 metres

Land below 100 metres

Main limestone areas

1

2

North Pennines

4 3

Peak District

5   8

9

Mendips

6

10

7

0   100 km

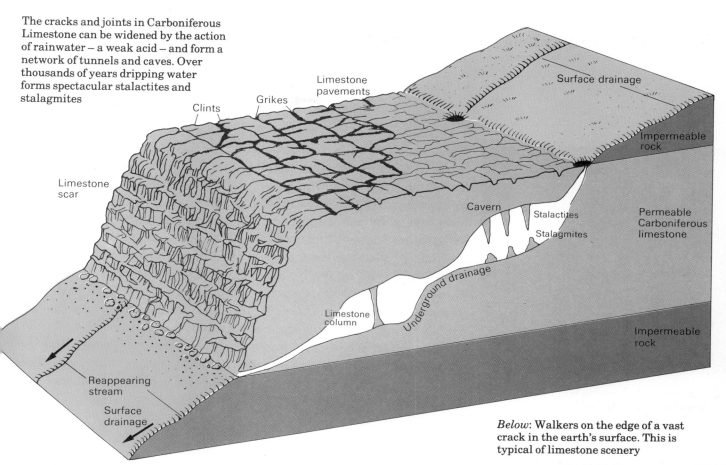

The cracks and joints in Carboniferous Limestone can be widened by the action of rainwater – a weak acid – and form a network of tunnels and caves. Over thousands of years dripping water forms spectacular stalactites and stalagmites

Limestone pavements

Clints

Grikes

Surface drainage

Limestone scar

Impermeable rock

Cavern

Stalactites

Stalagmites

Permeable Carboniferous limestone

Underground drainage

Limestone column

Impermeable rock

Reappearing stream

Surface drainage

Below: Walkers on the edge of a vast crack in the earth's surface. This is typical of limestone scenery

Many people who enjoy mountain and lake scenery keep to the main roads in the valleys or tracks in the hills. Others enjoy the exciting but dangerous sport of rock climbing – dangerous, that is, if proper care is not taken. Equally exciting – and dangerous, unless properly clothed, equipped and prepared – is potholing. Potholers explore underground tunnels and caves. Not all rocks have caves but in some, such as the limestones of the Carboniferous age, the underground passages can be spectacular. Limestone caves such as those at Cheddar Gorge attract thousands of sightseers, but potholers like to get away from crowds into the deeper, smaller and usually more difficult tunnels. Accidents can easily happen, and rescues are difficult. There is always the danger that the level of water will rise rapidly after a rainstorm, trapping people underground.

Below: Potholer in action. Potholing is a popular but dangerous sport

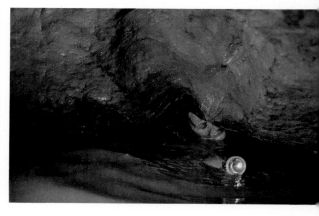

1 What are some of the weather hazards of mountain and upland areas? You will have already come across some of the clues in this book – mention them in your answer.

2 Imagine you are climbing, hill walking or potholing. Describe your feelings as you pause to look around you.

3 Suggest some of the dangers of potholing. What would be sensible clothing to wear and precautions to take before going into tunnels and caves?

4 From an atlas name the mountain and upland areas numbered 1–10 on the map. Give the name of one area with carboniferous limestone rocks.

5 Why do you think mountain and upland areas, so far from the centres of population, are so attractive to people?

The Lake District

The Lake District is the name given to the area of mountains and lakes in Cumbria in the north-west of England. The details of the landscape have been caused by ice sheets and glaciers that once covered the area. During the Ice Age, when much of northern Britain was covered by a huge ice-sheet, an ice cap covered the top of these mountains. Tongues of ice, known as glaciers, moved outwards from the centre following the course of the main river valleys. As the ice moved down valley it plucked away fragments of rock and debris. These became embedded in the ice and together the ice and rock fragments wore away the floor and sides of the valley. As the ice melted near its snout, or end, the rocks and stones were deposited in great mounds. When the climate of Britain became warmer, the ice sheets and glaciers melted, leaving U-shaped, ice-carved valleys. The long narrow lakes are just one of the results of this combined ice erosion and deposition.

Climbing near Lake Thirlmere

Right: Wastwater in the Lake District. Compare the shape of the valley with the diagram of the U-shaped valley on the opposite page.

Because it is attractive to so many people a large part of it is now a National Park where people may go to enjoy the scenery and take part in outdoor activities. The land is still farmed and people live and work in villages and small towns. There may also be some mining or forestry work. But being in a National Park means that special permission has to be given by the Park authorities before anything new is started. So no new buildings are put up, new industries started, roads built, mines or quarries opened or lakes turned into reservoirs without such permission. It is hoped that in this way full use can be made of the land without it being spoilt for those who enjoy it now – or for their children in the future.

1   Look at the map of the Lake District and at the diagram. Note the shape of the lakes and suggest reasons for this.
2   Name or draw two ways in which hills and mountains are shown on the map.
3   Draw a picture of the Wastwater photograph and label to show rugged peak, lake, steep slopes. Add labels for any other interesting features.
4   Make a list of all the leisure activities that could be followed out of doors in any area of the Lake District except for the towns. Name a likely place for each to happen.

Boats on one of the lakes: an example of recreation in the Lake District National Park

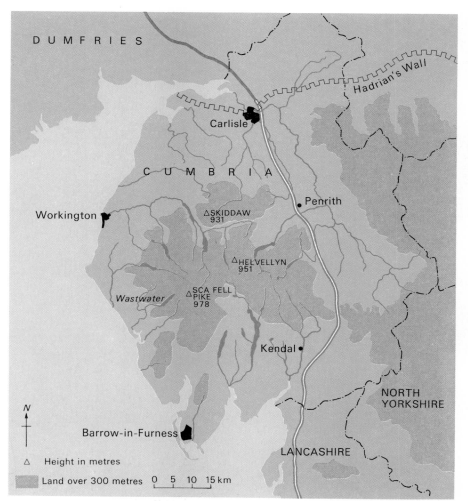

(a) River and tributary before glaciation

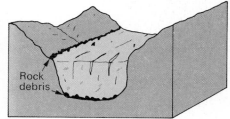

(b) Main valley filled by glacier

Rock debris

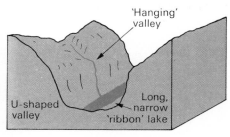

(c) River valley after erosion by glacier

'Hanging' valley

U-shaped valley

Long, narrow 'ribbon' lake

The process of glaciation. A river and tributary (a) is filled by a glacier moving down the slope of the main valley and (b) when the glacier retreats, this leaves a characteristic 'U-shaped' valley and a 'hanging' valley, often with a long narrow lake in the bed of the main valley

Left: The Lake District

39

Beside the sea

Yachts in full sail

Most people enjoy the sea, and like visiting the coast. In some places there are cliffs. These vary in height, shape and colour – from towering grey granite and steep white chalk cliffs to more gently sloping red sandstone. Elsewhere around the coast are low gentle beaches of sand or pebbles. As the tide rises and falls, and as the waves wash up and down the beach, the sand, shingle, pebbles and any other debris is moved and sorted along the beach.

In the photographs the sea looks calm with the waves gently washing the shore. During stormy weather, though, the waves and the stones and boulders they carry will pound against the cliff face and wear it away. Bits of cliff will fall into the sea. The weaker parts will be scooped out to form caves and bays while the more resistant will jut out into the sea to form headlands or small islands, called stacks. During strong winds all is noise and violence.

Small caravan site near sandstone cliffs

Tobermoray. About seven hundred people live in Tobermoray on the island of Mull off the west coast of Scotland, but many more visit it each year

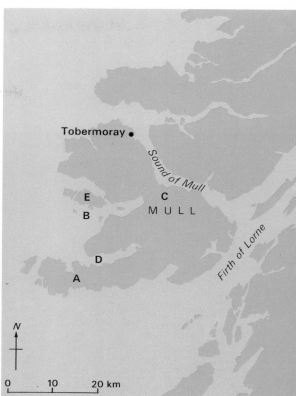

Fishing villages have existed around the coast ever since the land was first settled. Some harbours are still used by fishing boats, but many of the boats these days are dinghies, yachts and pleasure boats used by visiting tourists. A lot of the houses in the village will offer bed and breakfast accommodation, and there will be one or two hotels. Where there is an attractive stretch of coast but no village or town then people may stay at camp or caravan sites. This is a small one. Some are almost ten times bigger. It is easy to imagine the caravan site spreading into adjoining fields.

There are many ways of spending leisure time at the coast such as walking along the beach or cliff-top paths looking at the scenery, swimming, sailing or collecting such things as shells and pebbles. Sailing has become so popular that some towns have built marinas – special harbours for yachts and pleasure craft.

Fish and chips and a good read. A quiet holiday at Tobermoray

1. What do you think the caravan site was once used for? What will have been added to improve it as a caravan site? What are the dangers of too many caravans in a site like this?
2. Describe a holiday you have taken at the coast other than at a big town or holiday camp. What was the coast like? What was there to do? If you have never been to such a place choose one of those shown here and imagine what a visit would be like.
3. Suggest some of the ways in which Tobermoray might encourage tourists to visit it. What are some of the ways in which it could be spoilt by tourists?
4. Trace or draw the map of Mull but replace the letters with one of these words – island; sea lock or inlet; peninsula; isthmus; bay. Put into a short sentence what each word describes.

Seaside resort

Not everyone wants a quiet time at the coast, nor to stay at a caravan site. This is why seaside resorts are so popular – there is something for everybody. There are the simple pleasures of the beach. Children usually enjoy playing on the sand or paddling in the sea or running about making as much noise as they want. Their parents and grandparents want to sit in the sun and the sea breeze, or walk in the parks and gardens. But for a change a visit can be made to the fun fair and amusement arcades. These will be on the pier if the town is lucky enough to have one. In the evenings there are theatres, cinemas, clubs, discos and dance halls to relax in and be entertained. Unlike the quiet seaside village all is bustle, crowds, noise and excitement.

Many visitors to Blackpool or other resorts will be day trippers who have come by coach or car. Others will have come for a week or more – probably for the annual family holiday. This is why there are many hotels and boarding houses. Those nearest the beach are

Blackpool beach

Right: Blackpool from the air. Notice its beach, pier and tower

usually the most expensive. There are dozens of restaurants and cafes as well as lots of hot-dog, hamburger and ice-cream stalls.

Most people take seaside holidays in the summer. The seaside town is full during the summer months, but in the winter the hotels, boarding houses, car and coach parks are empty and there are far fewer jobs to be done.

Close by some seaside towns you may find a holiday camp. These camps have been built to provide everything that might be needed on a holiday. They provide chalets to sleep in, dining rooms and all sorts of places for recreation and entertainment.

In the past it was difficult to reach the seaside and only wealthy people could manage it. Then came the railways and coaches that allowed millions of day-trippers to visit the seaside from the big industrial towns. Then more and more used their own cars as means of getting to the seaside. The most important change in recent years has been that many people take holidays abroad on package tours. It may be as quick and cheap to go to Spain, say, as somewhere in Britain. Even so, the seaside resort is still very popular.

1 Make a class survey to find out which seaside resorts in Britain have been visited. Make a note of the resorts that have been visited most often. Are these resorts close to your home town compared with other resorts? Write an account of 'A perfect day at the seaside', either from memory or as you imagine it would be.

2 Find out from a) parents and b) grandparents or other older people about visiting the seaside when they were children. How did they get there, how long did they stay, where did they stay, what did they do?

3 What are some of the buildings found only in seaside resorts? What land uses can you think of that are not so important in inland towns of the same size? Where are these special seaside-town buildings and land uses likely to be?

4 Design a poster for a seaside resort of your choice showing its attractions.

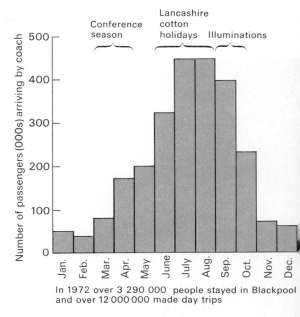

In 1972 over 3 290 000 people stayed in Blackpool and over 12 000 000 made day trips

Seasonal changes at a seaside resort: monthly arrivals by coach at Blackpool

The site of Blackpool

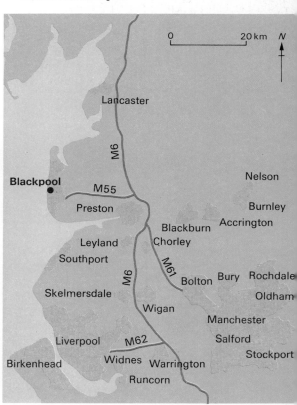

The famous Blackpool Illuminations

43

Village

Limestone and thatch houses. Hodcote, Gloucestershire

Flint and tile houses, Hambleden, Oxfordshire. Flints are stones found left behind when chalk rock has been worn away

Less than two hundred years ago far more people lived on farms and in villages than lived in towns. Many of the villagers would work on nearby farms. Other villagers would be craftsmen such as black-smiths who made farm equipment and shoed the horses and millers who made flour from the cereal crop. Among the buildings in the village would be cottages for the workers and their families. There would also probably be an inn, a small church or chapel with a house for the parson or priest, and a shop or two. Most of these would be around a village green. In some villages there would be a large house set in its own grounds which belonged to the local squire or landowner.

People were unable to travel far. They could only go on foot or by horse and cart. Their main journeys would be to the local town on market days. Some people never went much further than that in their lifetime. Most of the things the villagers needed were grown or made from local materials or bought in the local market town. It was a fairly simple life.

There were many villages in Britain, but they were small and scattered. Most of them were found in places which were suitable for farming. Exceptions included fishing villages around the coast and some mining villages. Even within farming areas not all sites were equally good for a village. There was need for water, so they were usually found near streams or where water could be got from wells. They kept away from wet or marshy areas, or where the land was too steep.

Brick and tile houses, Finchingfield, Essex. Bricks are made from clay

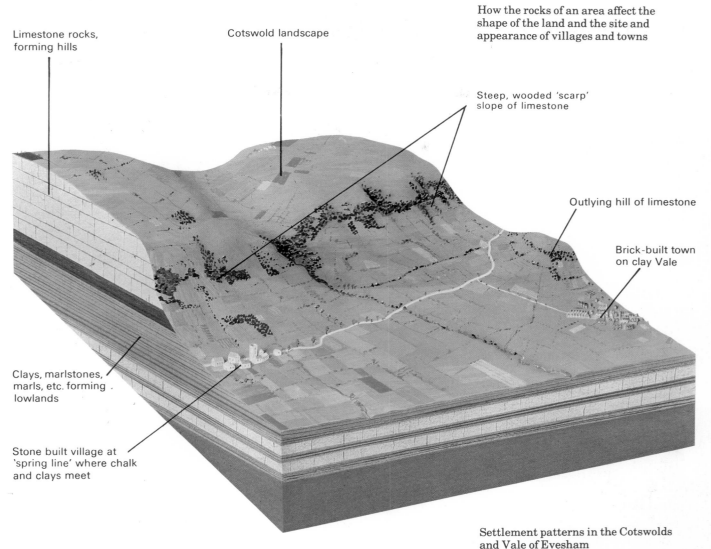

Limestone rocks, forming hills

Cotswold landscape

How the rocks of an area affect the shape of the land and the site and appearance of villages and towns

Steep, wooded 'scarp' slope of limestone

Outlying hill of limestone

Brick-built town on clay Vale

Clays, marlstones, marls, etc. forming lowlands

Stone built village at 'spring line' where chalk and clays meet

Some villages grew into larger market towns. This was likely to happen at villages where several roads met, or where a river could be crossed. It was once important to be able to defend these towns, so they were often found in loops of rivers that formed a sort of moat. Many had walls and castles built for defense. There were fewer market towns than villages, and they were more widely spaced.

1 List the jobs that were done in the village in the past. What were some of the reasons why the villagers needed to go to their local market town?
2 Write a short account about life in the village several hundred years ago. Say what you think you would have liked or disliked about it.
3 What buildings mentioned in the description can be seen in the villages in the photographs? What makes the villages look different from a new housing estate? Why do the houses in the three areas look different?
4 Copy the map and add the words – limestone hills; steep scarp slope; outlying hill capped with limestone; clay and marlstone lowland.
5 How many towns are there on the map and how many smaller villages? What do you notice about the sites of the towns? Why are the villages in long lines on the limestone but scattered on the clay vale? Why is there a long line of villages between A and B?

Settlement patterns in the Cotswolds and Vale of Evesham

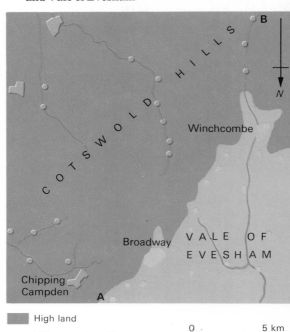

B

COTSWOLD HILLS

N

Winchcombe

Broadway

VALE OF EVESHAM

Chipping Campden

A

High land

Villages and small towns

0   5 km

Changing village

Right: Axbridge. The old village High Street and square, and new housing estate. The new by-pass on the left of the picture was built on the old railway and the station can be seen half-way up the picture

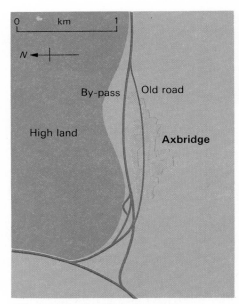

The site of Axbridge in Somerset

There have been many changes in village life and in the look of villages and small towns in recent times. Older people will often say how different things were when they were children. Those who lived in these settlements several centuries ago would be amazed at what has happened to most of them.

Some villages have grown into large towns. The old village buildings can sometimes be seen near the centre of these towns even today. They are often regarded as important because they remind us of the past, and efforts are made to conserve these old parts of towns.

Some villages have been swallowed up as a town or city expanded. In London, for example, there are many suburbs that still have the look and feel of a village, even though they are surrounded by modern houses and not open fields. Hampstead, Dulwich and Wimbledon are examples of this.

The roads through old villages were never intended for motor traffic. They are often narrow and twisting. As more and more cars and heavy lorries used village roads they not only made them unpleasant places to live in because of the noise and fumes. They also caused damage to streets and buildings and were a danger to pedestrians. To avoid this by-passes have been built around some villages and small towns. People who want to can still drive into the village, but those who only want to pass through now have a much quicker journey and cause much less of a nuisance. The life of many a village has been saved by building a by-pass.

Many people like the atmosphere of a village, but are unable to earn a living in them because of the nature of their jobs. This is where the car has ensured the survival of many villages. Such people live in the village and travel to work in the nearest town or city by car or by

Earl planning to give away a spare village

Left: Extract from 'Guardian' newspaper, 14 August 1979

A council in Yorkshire is considering accepting an entire village as a gift from Lord Fitzwilliam, one of the country's wealthiest landowners.

The earl, who is 75, has asked Rotherham borough council if it wants to take over the village of Scholes with its overgrown gardens, dilapidated houses and chemical lavatories.

Little has been done to maintain the once picturesque village over the past few years. There is no main drainage system in the area and the village school, post office and sole shop have long since closed.

Most of the villagers, who pay very small rents to the earl's estate, are in favour of the plan, although some are concerned that the council might expand the village and spoil its character.

Kew 'village' in London

train. New estates of houses are built by private property developers or local authorities for these commuters. For people who work in the village, the car is a great advantage for shopping in the nearby town. In many cases there are two villages and two sets of villagers – the old and the new.

1 Compare the houses on the outskirts of Axbridge in the distance with those near the village square and along the main street.
2 Say a few words about the site of Axbridge.
3 Look at the map of Sunningwell. Choose the church, inn or vehicle repair works and say if you think it is in a good or bad place for the villagers. The new building (number 3) is the new school. Why is it on the edge of the village? Is it well located for the village?
4 Do you think it is worth trying to conserve old village features in small country towns or in big cities? If not, why not?

Sunningwell village, Oxfordshire. Age and use of buildings

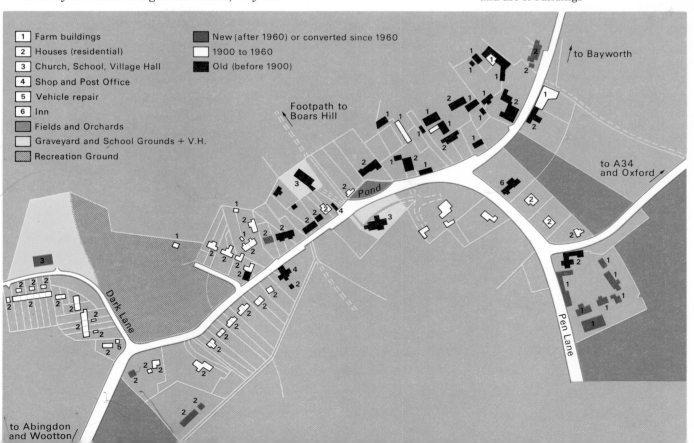

1 Farm buildings
2 Houses (residential)
3 Church, School, Village Hall
4 Shop and Post Office
5 Vehicle repair
6 Inn
Fields and Orchards
Graveyard and School Grounds + V.H.
Recreation Ground

New (after 1960) or converted since 1960
1900 to 1960
Old (before 1900)

Capital city

Commuters at Farnborough

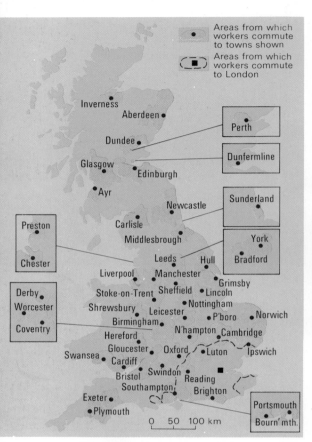

Commuter areas of the main towns in Britain

The people on the station at Farnborough are waiting for the early morning train to take them to London. They travel to the city to work and they are called 'commuters'. Each working day London's railways carry about six million people from home to work and back again. If a line were drawn around all the towns and villages from where people travel to work in London we could see the 'commuter area' for the city. A rough idea of the area can be seen on the map.

London also has a 'catchment' area or a 'sphere of influence' for its shops and offices and for its goods and services. To obtain some sorts of goods, or to have treatment at a special hospital, or to see a leading solicitor or lawyer you will almost certainly have to go to a big city. Since London is by far the biggest city in Britain it is not suprising that its catchment area or sphere of influence for goods and services includes most of the country. Most people who work in London, though, will live within an hour or two of the city.

If you travel on a London commuter train or bus at the end of the day, you will see that many people will be reading a London evening paper. The London evening papers carry a lot of national and international news, but also a great deal that interests mainly those who live or work in the city or the towns within its sphere of influence. These people will also probably watch the independent TV programmes for the London area and listen to one of the local radio stations. Local newspapers, radio and television have spheres of influence for information, news and entertainment.

Central London: recent building development

Right, below: Tourists looking across the Thames to the Houses of Parliament

London is not only the biggest city in the United Kingdom (that is, England, Scotland, Wales and Northern Ireland), it is also the capital of this country. The Houses of Parliament, where men and women elected to govern the country meet and work are in London. Here you will also find many of the main offices of the civil servants who help carry out the laws passed in Parliament. In this sense the sphere of influence for political purposes is the whole country. This is what being a capital city really means.

For some people in Wales, Scotland and the North of England, London is a far-away city that they seldom visit. They would rather see a city closer to them taking on many of the functions of a capital city. This demand for 'devolution' is especially strong in Wales and Scotland for historic reasons, and has been recognised to some extent. Many central government activities now take place outside London.

1 What is the furthest distance commuters travel into a city other than London? What determines how far people will commute? What is the furthest distance any member of your family travels to work each day?
2 Where would you be likely to commute to work if you lived somewhere between Bristol and Gloucester? What would help you decide what to do?
3 Shrewsbury is a much smaller town than Liverpool, but the distance travelled by commuter is about the same. Try to explain this.
4 Which town or city sphere of influence are you under for **a**) grocery shopping, **b**) furniture shopping, **c**) going to a theatre, **d**) watching a First Division football game **e**) getting an evening newspaper?

London, capital of the United Kingdom

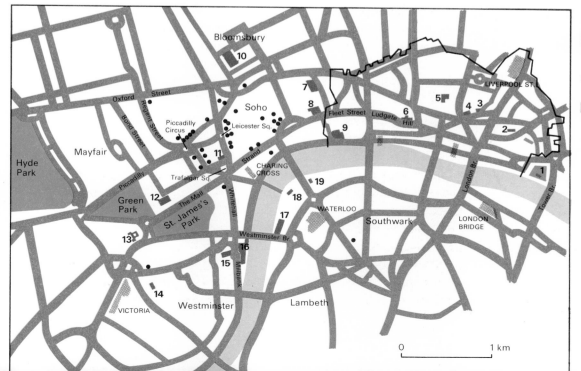

Boundary of City of London
Park
Main-line railway station
Main thoroughfare
• Theatre
1 Tower
2 Lloyds
3 Stock Exchange
4 Bank of England
5 Guildhall
6 St. Paul's Cathedral
7 Lincoln's Inn
8 Law Courts
9 Temple
10 British Museum
11 National Gallery
12 St. James's Palace
13 Buckingham Palace
14 Westminster Cathedral
15 Westminster Abbey
16 Houses of Parliament
17 County Hall
18 Festival Hall
19 National Theatre

0   1 km

City, town and village

Settlement pattern

Right: Norwich is the County Town of Norfolk

The centre of the small town of Holt in Norfolk showing how busy such a market centre can be

Norwich is the County Town of Norfolk. It is the 'capital' of the county in the same way that London is the capital of the United Kingdom. Here is the County Hall where the men and women elected to govern the county meet. You can compare county councillors with Members of Parliament. But the decisions they make only affect the people of Norfolk. Here also are many of the offices of the local authority workers such as the people who run the planning, education, highways and social service departments. They try to carry out the decisions made by the councillors, who have been elected by the people in Norfolk who voted in the local elections.

Norwich was once the second largest city in England, but now it has a population of about 180 000, which means it is not in the 'top twenty' British cities as far as population goes. There is a nine

Cley-next-the-Sea, a village on the coast of Norfolk. Many such small villages are built on slightly higher ground to avoid flooding

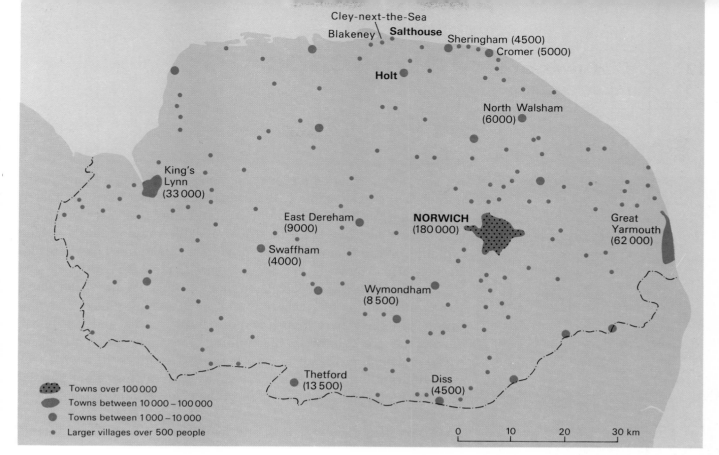

City, town and village in Norfolk

hundred-year-old castle, a cathedral and a new university. Like all big cities there are many shops and offices in the Central Business District, as well as cinemas, theatres and museums.

There are a number of medium-sized towns scattered about the county. Holt is a good example of one of these towns. It is located in north Norfolk. Its shopping centre is very much smaller than that of Norwich. But a lot of people from surrounding villages use Holt to shop for things they cannot get in their village shop, such as clothes and electrical goods.

These villages are both inland and on the coast. Those on the coast used to be mainly fishing villages, but nowadays they attract many tourists. The harbours of places such as Blakeney are full of pleasure boats as well as small fishing craft. Here and there, though, as at Cley-next-the-Sea, the original character of the small village has not been greatly changed.

1 What are some of the shops and services that you are likely to get in Holt that you will not get in Cley-next-the-Sea? What are some that you are likely to get in Norwich but not in Holt?
2 Although the number of farm workers and fisherman have declined in recent years, the population of many of the villages has increased. Try to explain this.
3 Draw an imaginary map of an island to show the pattern of settlements of different size – village, small town, medium-sized town, city. Add a scale line and a key to say how many people live in each settlement.
4 What do you notice about the number of settlements a) between 500 and 1 000, b) between 1 000 and 10 000, c) between 10 000 and 100 000, d) over 100 000 in Norfolk?

The graph shows how the number of settlements varies with size. There are a lot of small settlements but only a few big ones.

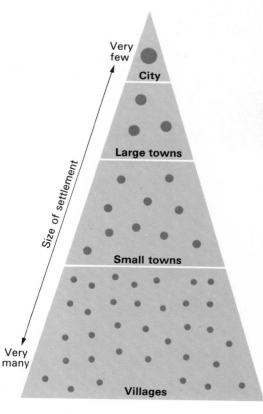

51

Townscape

A Welsh coal-mining town

No two towns or cities are exactly the same, although many towns may look the same at first. Places such as modern town centres, or areas of terraced housing, or new estates may look very much the same wherever they are. But sooner or later you will find a special building, or street, or open space, or view that is unlike anywhere else in the world. You know you are in a special place.

The look of a town depends on many things. Its site – the shape and position of the land where it started as a small village or a new town – will play a part. Some towns are built on hills, and as you look down some streets between the buildings you can see other streets, or woods and fields rising up on the other side. This gives the town a 'feel' very different from that in a flat, level area. Many towns built on flat land are by a river, and the shape of the river will affect the 'feel' of the town.

Towns near the coast look and feel different from those inland. Coming into the town you can first smell the sea and hear the seagulls. Then you may catch glimpses of the sea with its beaches or cliffs. On the sea front there will be lines of big hotels and theatres and probably a pier that makes it look unlike any inland town.

Cardiff Docks

Royal Crescent, Bath

Durham: a cathedral, county and university town. Each of the four photographs shows a distinctive townscape determined by age and function

The jobs done by people in three different sorts of town

		A	B	C
1	Manufacturing (working in factories)	17%	21%	43%
2	Distributive (shops, etc)	22%	15%	18%
3	Professional services (doctors, lawyers, etc)	9%	26%	9%
4	Other services (waiters, etc)	33%	21%	14%

The age of a town also affects its appearance. This is not only because different building materials were used, but also because new estates and New Towns and shopping centres tend to be planned and very regular. Older towns usually grew up without such planning – although the photograph of Bath on page 52 reminds us that in the past many private builders tried hard to plan their buildings to fit into the landscape and with each other.

Not all coastal towns are seaside resorts. One of the most striking townscapes is that of cranes towering over the docks and shipyards of large ports. Factories and power stations sometimes stand out as much as church towers in other towns. The jobs people do and the buildings they work in have a big impact on the look of a town.

1   Say a few words about the site of Durham. From your atlas say where Durham, Bath and Cardiff are located in Britain.
2   Towns have a different 'feel' or character. Put into words your feelings about Bath and the coal-mining town. Do the same for Blackpool (page 42) and Leicester (page 76).
3   Although a wide range of jobs are done in most towns, each tends to specialise in one sort of work. Look at the three towns in the table and the jobs done in each. Say which you think is an industrial town with lots of factories, which a seaside town and which a University and county town. Then name an example from this book of each of these three types.

Streetscape

Cardiff Bus Station. It is the activity of the people and the buses that makes a place like this interesting

Streets within towns are as different from each other as towns are. Not all places look the same or make us feel the same. Some are exciting and some boring. Some make us pleased and some make us miserable. Some streets have great blocks of offices, shops or flats towering on both sides. This is a good way of using expensive land – to put the streets on top of each other! But a lot of people find high-rise buildings unpleasant. They are so big that they make them feel small and insignificant. High buildings shut out the sun. They often cause winds to be blustery in the narrow streets. Town centres where there are high buildings can be bleak and lonely places in the evenings when there are few people about and the shops and offices are closed.

Other kinds of street that produce very different kinds of feeling include; streets of old terraced houses, places where houses are jumbled up with factories, elegant Georgian crescents such as those in Bath or new estates where all the houses are fairly small and look the same. They feel different partly because the buildings are made of different materials. The older terraced houses are likely to be made of brick and tile and the newer flats of concrete, steel and glass.

Terraced houses on both sides of a street in a coal mining town in South Wales

'Streets in the sky'. High rise flats at Paddington in London

High Holborn in London from the air

Left above: Another London scene from the air: Petticoat Lane

The different feeling is partly due to the different size of the buildings and the way they are clustered together or spaced out. Most people do not like buildings to be too packed together, yet some of the bleakest places are open windswept estates on the outskirts of towns where there is plenty of open space. Many think that what makes a place interesting is its small scale and variety – the changes in the look of the different buildings, the mixture of open streets and narrow, twisting alleyways running off them. A lot will also depend how noisy or dirty the street is. Few people like streets full of rubbish on the pavements, graffiti on the walls, broken fences and windows or junk and abandoned cars in the road.

Above all it is what is going on that makes a street interesting. Streets with people going in and out of shops or trading at a street market. Streets with children playing, people sitting and looking, meeting friends, having a chat. These are very different from the lonely streets in a big estate or surrounding a tower block.

A street in a wealthy part of London

1 Look at the three streets in the photographs. Choose two. How do the buildings and the way they are laid out differ? Which do you like and which do you dislike? Say why. (Talk about the outsides, not the insides of the buildings).
2 Choose a street in a housing or residential area and one in a shopping area that you know. Either draw a labelled sketch of each or put into words what you like or dislike about the streets.
3 Why do you think some people do not care about the streets they use – why do they drop litter, leave rubbish, break things or scribble graffiti on walls? Do you think it matters?
4 How do you think people could be persuaded not to do the things mentioned in the question above?

Early beginnings

A map of Bristol drawn about one hundred years before the map below

Most cities are very old. They may have started as villages and small towns hundreds of years ago and grown to their present size over a long period of time. We saw what London looked like almost 2 000 years ago in the drawing on page 9. In very old cities and towns like this the buildings are of different ages and styles.

The place where the city started, which is called its 'site' is usually in or near the present City Centre. There were probably very good reasons why the first site was chosen, though we can rarely be absolutely certain what these were. Near the original site is where the oldest buildings are likely to be found. Not many of the very old buildings are likely to remain today. Perhaps there will be a bit of the city wall or castle or church. Nearly all the ordinary houses will have vanished long ago. We can find out about the past of a city from old buildings or the remains of them that still exist. We can also learn a lot from old maps, drawings and photographs.

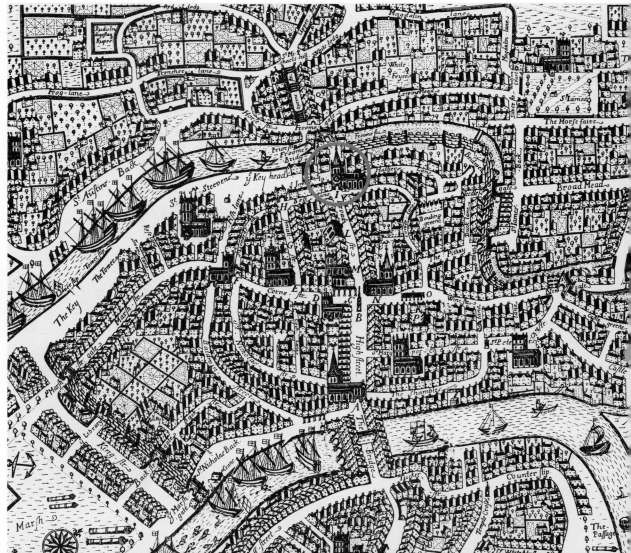

Millerd's plan of Bristol, 1673. The same church is circled on the photographs opposite, and on page 58

The early beginnings of Bristol are not known, but there are signs that a town called Brigstow existed over 1 300 years ago. This Saxon name means 'a meeting place near the bridge'. The first bridge is thought to have been in the same place as the one shown on the map. The site of Brigstow was on slightly higher ground between the River Avon and the smaller River Frome. We cannot be certain why this site was chosen, but can guess that the high ground protected the settlement from flooding and was a good place from which to view the surrounding land. The Saxon settlers built walls around the settlement at an early stage. When the Normans invaded the area they built a castle on the site. The castle had been pulled down by the time Millerd drew his map.

Bristol became a large port. Merchants in the city traded with West Africa and the West Indies and became very wealthy. Goods were taken to Africa, slaves transported from there across the Atlantic Ocean to the West Indies and tobacco, cocoa and other goods imported into the city. The town grew in size, and had many factories. As more people came to live and work there, new houses had to be built. Many old buildings were destroyed by bombs during the last war and by redevelopment since. But there are still about 60 timber-framed buildings built before 1700 in the central area, and many more from the following centuries a little further out from the centre.

Redcliffe Street, 1825: the curved street at the bottom of Millerd's map

Left, below: Wine Street, looking towards Corn Street, 1913

Below: Between Wine Street and Broadmead, 1921. Chocolate and cigarette factories were then in the centre of the city. Why were these products made in Bristol?

1 What are the signs on the map by Millerd that Bristol once had a castle and was a large port and market town, and was quite wealthy? What do you like or dislike about this sort of map?

2 Draw a simple map of the early site of Bristol and label to show the features that you think made it a good place to start a town.

3 Imagine you were a visitor to Bristol in the 1920s. Describe your impressions of the area around Wine Street and Broadmead.

4 Work out from the table how many extra people had to be housed between 1800–1850; 1850–1900; 1900–1950. When was the greatest increase?

Population of Bristol 1800–1950

1800	70 000
1850	150 000
1900	333 000
1950	443 000

Central Business District

The street running through the centre of the photograph is Corn Street leading into Wine Street. To the right is the River Avon and one end of Bristol Bridge while to the left, near the edge of the photograph, is the street called Broadmead. The River Frome, full of ships on Millerd's map, cannot be seen. Nowadays it flows through drains beneath the grass covered open space in the front of the photograph.

The centre is a good place to have offices and shops serving the whole city and the surrounding areas, since it is usually the easiest place to get to. Because a lot of firms want to be there, though, the value of the land is high and rates and rents are also expensive. So buildings are built upwards to save ground space.

The shops are usually large, and include chain and department stores such as Boots, Sainsburys and Marks and Spencers. Here will be the Headquarters of banks, building societies and big companies, and very often the offices of the local district and county councils. Because so much business is carried on here, such areas are often called the Central Business District. The name is not strictly true,

City centre by day (*above*) and the same area in the evening (*below*)

Right: Bristol: the Central Business District. The same church is marked on Millerd's map and the early photographs

since there are often cinemas, restaurants, hotels, clubs, theatres and parks amongst the offices and shops.

Few people live in the city centre. Workers travel into and out of it each day. Traffic is a problem, especially during the rush hours when work starts and ends. The roads get jammed up, and the buses and suburban trains are packed. It is difficult to find places to park a car. City centres are busy, bustling places during most days, but are often empty, quiet and lonely – apart from the restaurants and theatres and clubs – in the evenings and at week-ends.

As the Central Business District expands more and more people move out of the inner city and live in the suburbs. In some cities efforts are being made to get people to move back into the city centre by providing inexpensive housing amongst the office buildings.

1   Look at the part of Bristol around Wine Street in the 1920s. This part of Bristol was badly damaged by bombs during the Second World War. What changes have happened? What is the area used for now?
2   How is the shortage and high cost of land in the city centre shown by the new buildings put up in central Bristol? If land is scarce, is it sensible to give so much space to parkland?
3   Look at the table of population change. Name three 'wards' or areas with the biggest % loss. Where are they? Why have these wards lost population?
4   On a map of the central area of your town or city try and draw a line around the big offices, shops, hotels and places of entertainment. Add any central bus or railway stations and show the main car parks. Give a title.

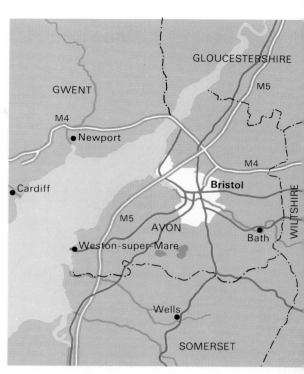

Bristol and its relationship to its surrounding area

Percentage population change in Bristol 1951–1971

Avon	+ 3.7
Bedminster	− 23.5
Bishopston	− 15.9
Bishopsworth	+ 587.5
Brislington	− 3.8
Cabot	− 40.1
Clifton	− 6.3
District	− 10.6
Durdham	− 0.6
Easton	− 39.1
Eastville	− 14.9
Henbury	+ 118.2
Hengrove	− 9.8
Hillfields	− 17.0
Horfield	− 14.8
Knowle	− 18.7
Redland	− 6.7
St George East	+ 2.8
St George West	− 34.3
St Paul	− 50.3
St Phillip & Jacob	− 67.5
Somerset	− 11.6
Southmead	− 3.4
Southville	− 32.0
Stapleton	− 6.9
Stockwood	+ 161.5
Westbury-on-Trym	+ 27.6
Windmill Hill	− 39.2

The wards of Bristol

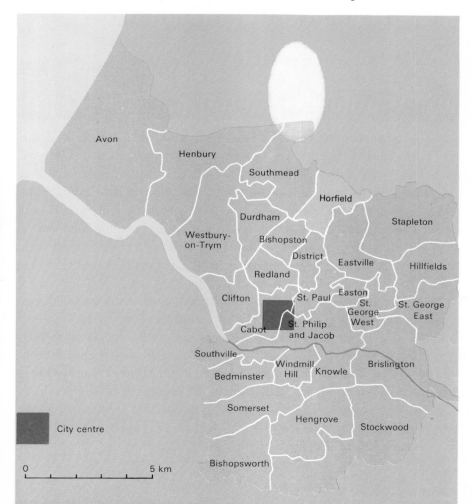

City centre

0 _____ 5 km

Inner city

A street in the older inner city area of
Blackburn

A redeveloped high-rise area in Salford,
near Manchester

In the older parts of our cities there are thousands of streets like the one in Blackburn. Not all are as hilly, but otherwise they look very much the same. Long brick lines of two or three storied terraced houses face each other across the street. Front doors lead straight on to the pavement and the back garden is likely to be very small and narrow. These houses were built over a hundred years ago. They were intended for factory workers when standards of living were much lower than they are today. They were built near the factories to make it easy for the workers to get to work.

There are no garages – people didn't have cars when these houses were built. The bigger houses are often sub-divided into flats. There is likely to be a corner shop nearby with a small parade of shops selling all sorts of everyday needs a short distance away on a busier street. Nearby will be a school for young children. Older pupils usually have to travel further to a secondary school. There could be a church or chapel on the street, although it might now be used for non-religious purposes. There may be a small park, but lack of grass, trees and open space is common in inner cities.

Gasometers and factories loom over the houses in the Blackburn street. Factories railway tracks, stations, small workshops and garages and perhaps a canal may all be mixed in with the homes. Unfortunately many of the inner city factories have had to close and there may be few jobs in the area.

Because the inner areas of cities were often very old and worn out, and the houses lacked 'amenities' like bathrooms and inside lavatories, the local housing authorities have knocked them down and put up new estates. These have usually been high-rise flats, although nowadays it is as common to find the old houses have been kept but the insides improved.

Since jobs are not easy to get, many young families have moved out to find work elsewhere. Immigrant families, particularly from the West Indies, Pakistan and India who find it difficult to get homes elsewhere have concentrated in the older inner city areas or nearby suburbs.

1 Choose either the street scene in Blackburn or the redevelopment in Salford. Describe it and compare it with the area that you live in.
2 Look at the map. Count the number of houses within the kilometre square. What is the density of housing in that kilometre? If each house was in two flats with one family to each, what would be the density of families per square kilometre?
3 How do the amenities of the two areas shown in the table differ?
4 What do you think makes a) a house or flat, b) a street or area, a pleasant place to live in? What spoils it?

An example of change in the inner city. Large office blocks replace old housing and homes

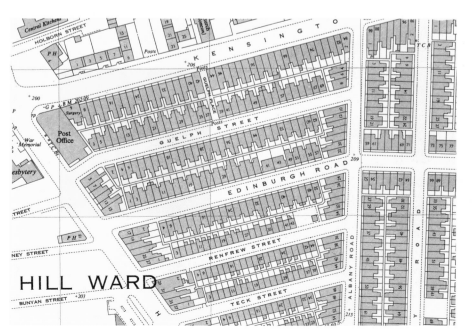

HILL WARD

Household amenities in inner city and suburban areas

	Own	Shared	None
Inner city area			
Hot water tap	60.0%	10.0%	30.0%
Fixed bath	67.5%	5.0%	27.5%
Inside W.C.	47.5%	5.0%	47.5%
Suburban area			
Hot water tap	99.2%	0.8%	0.0%
Fixed bath	99.2%	0.8%	0.0%
Inside W.C.	99.2%	0.8%	0.2%

The Low Hill area of inner Liverpool

Outer city

A typical pair of semi-detached suburban houses

Over the last sixty years hundreds of thousands of homes have been built outside the inner city, and the cities have expanded into the surrounding countryside. These suburbs are very different from place to place, and almost always unlike the old terraced housing of the inner area.

More and more people have wanted to own their own house, not rent it from a private landlord or the local council. Some have been able to do so by borrowing money from a Building Society. These owner-occupiers have wanted more space, and so the builders have put up detached and semi-detached houses with big gardens at the rear and smaller ones at the front. The density of housing has been lower than where there are lots of terraced houses. The rooms have been usually larger than most terraced houses, and they have had bathrooms and inside lavatories, and usually a hot water system.

Streets in the suburbs are often lined with trees. There are many parks, playing fields, tennis courts and golf courses. There are very few corner shops, but spaced at intervals are small shopping parades. There are churches, chapels, halls and schools, but very few factories, except on special industrial estates.

The people who own or are buying their homes in the suburbs tend to work in offices, banks and shops, or are professional people, such as doctors. They usually travel some distance to work by car or train. Most of these houses have garages.

Suburban townscape from the air

Right: The Westbury-on-Trym area of Bristol

Part of Kirkby, a new housing area on the outskirts of Liverpool

Local housing authorities have also built council houses for renting (and sometimes for sale) in the suburbs and on the edge of cities. Kirkby on the edge of Liverpool is an example of a local council estate. Costs have to be kept down so, although the houses or flats are themselves quite reasonable, there isn't enough money to provide the public transport, shops, play areas and places of entertainment that people on these estates need. The houses may be good and there can be lots of open space. But the bustle, and friendliness that people need are sometimes lacking in all types of suburb.

1   Which of the things mentioned in the description of the suburbs can be seen in the two photographs?
2   Compare the map extract of the suburbs with the one of the inner city on the previous page. What are some of the differences in the two areas shown by the maps?
3   What are some of the differences between the housing in the photo of Kirkby and those in the suburban scenes?
4   Look at the graphs showing 'tenure' of housing – whether they are owned, rented from the council or from private landlords. What are the main differences in the two areas?

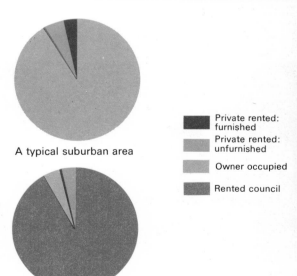

A typical suburban area

Private rented: furnished

Private rented: unfurnished

Owner occupied

Rented council

A typical outer city council estate

The proportion of homes owned or rented in two parts of a city

63

Corner shop and High Street

'Monument Street'. A cartoon of a London shopping area 150 years ago

A corner shop: in spite of its small size it is of very great importance to people who live in the nearby streets. It may stay open late and sell some goods on Sundays

A London street market

Most of the things we buy we get from shops. Newspapers and milk may be delivered to the house. Some things that have been ordered from advertisements in newspapers or catalogues will be sent by post or rail and van. Most often, though, we go to our local shops to get food or sweets or things that we need to buy quite often. For other things such as shoes, or tools, records or furniture that are bought less often we will either go to a specialist shop or a department store. We will probably go to several shops looking for the one with the best bargain which combines low cost with good quality.

From this you can tell that we use the word 'shop' to describe very different sorts of places. It can mean the small corner shop where we might go most days of the week, the supermarket where we do the weekly shopping for food or the big department store where we go to now and then to buy a refrigerator or record player.

Some shops sell a wide range of goods while others specialise. Specialist shops might sell meat, books, fashion clothes or cars, for example. We soon get to know these shops from their names and shop-front displays. Compared with the corner shop the department store will have much bigger and more expensive 'durable' items which last for a long time. People will travel to the department store from long distances, but most users of the corner shop will come from streets nearby. Some shops are part of a 'chain', which means that there will be similar ones with the same name in other parts of the town or in

A typical 'High Street' shopping centre, busy with people and traffic

Pedestrianised shopping precinct. People and traffic are kept apart

other towns around the country. Often big shops and stores with different names are owned by the same company.

Apart from the corner shop, most shops are clustered together usually with banks and offices. These clusters may be small 'parades' on estates or in the suburbs. Others are in 'High Streets' or in the centre of the town. In most towns and cities there will be a lot of shopping parades, a few larger High Street type of shopping areas and one big central shopping district.

Shopping centres are busy places – they have been built where they are because these are easy to get to by large numbers of people. Traffic can be dangerous, though, and traffic-free shopping precincts have been built in many places. Multi-storey car parks are nearly always found close to these precincts.

1. Make two lists, each with ten things you might buy. In the first put those things you buy very often, probably from a corner shop or supermarket. In the second put expensive 'durable' things your family might buy – but very rarely – from a department store.
2. Why is it a good idea to have a shop sited on the street corner? Why is it a good idea to locate the main shopping area at the centre of a town?
3. Why is it a good idea to cluster shops in a parade rather than spread them out amongst the houses?
4. How do shops advertise and 'sell' their goods? Draw or describe examples of local shop fronts and advertisements in the local paper.

Supermarket and hypermarket

A supermarket owned by a well-known company, in an older shopping centre

Inside a supermarket

Everyone is so used to supermarket shopping that it is hard to realise that few existed twenty years ago. In those days there were many small family-owned shops. Most of these have since closed down or been taken over by a supermarket company. A company may own supermarkets in dozens of towns, and several parts of one town.

In supermarkets there is 'self-service'. This means that customers select what they want from goods displayed on open shelves and pay at a check-out point. This makes them cheaper to run than those with lots of assistants to serve the customer. Big shops can also buy huge amounts of goods from the manufacturer or wholesaler at a lower price than if small amounts were ordered. So they can cut the price for the shopper.

Small self-service supermarkets can be found nowadays in most shopping parades. Bigger ones can be found in the suburban shopping streets and the biggest of all usually in the city centre. Since they rely on customers buying a lot of goods it is an advantage if cars can be parked near to the supermarket. This is often very difficult near the centre of towns or in busy streets because the space is needed for other purposes. One result is that really big supermarkets, called 'hypermarkets', are beginning to be built outside the towns where there is plenty of space for car parking. They serve people from a very wide area, but only those who are car owners or are on a convenient bus service.

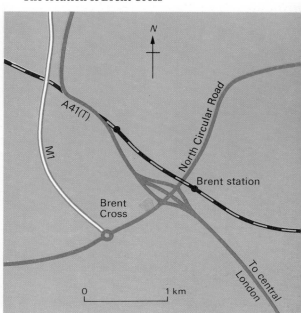

Brent Cross, London: an out-of-town shopping centre. Such centres depend on large numbers of customers being able to shop by car. The road is the west to east section of the North Circular road

The location of Brent Cross

An even newer development is the 'out-of-town' shopping centre. It is as though a complete shopping centre from a town centre were put in the suburbs where it can be easily reached by masses of people. Brent Cross in London is a good example. It was opened in 1976. It has two big Department stores, four chain stores and ninety separate shops. There is space for 4 000 cars, and on a Saturday more than 10 000 cars use it. People travel long distances to Brent Cross. But it doesn't take all that long because of the nearby motorways, very good bus services, and a railway station close by. Many people prefer travelling to Brent Cross rather than to Central London for durable goods and groceries.

1   What chain store is shown in the photograph opposite? Name well-known chain stores in your local shopping centre.
2   Imagine you are a) the owner, b) a customer. What are the advantages of the supermarket over the older sort of family shop with shop assistants?
3   There were only four or five hypermarkets in Britain in the late 1970s. If they are good ways of selling and buying goods, why were there so few? What are some of the difficulties in providing hypermarkets? What effect might a hypermarket have on the older shopping centres?
4   Look at the photograph and maps of Brent Cross. What is so good about the location for an out-of-town shopping centre? Why is it a sensible idea to make a map of the nearness to shops in terms of *time* to get there, not *distance*? Why can more people get to Brent Cross in a given time from the north than from the south? Why might fewer people from the south *want* to use Brent Cross even if it was as quick?

Car travelling times:
——— 10 mins
– – – 20 mins

Bus travelling times:
——— 10 mins
– – – 20 mins

The time taken to get to Brent Cross. Three out of four shoppers (75 per cent) travel by car. 250 000 people live within 25 minutes drive of this location

67

Factories and works

A small workshop in a garment factory (the 'rag trade'). Such workshops are often known as 'sweatshops' because the people in them work very long hours for very little money

Right: Women at work in a factory making high-value goods: washing machines and tumble dryers

An illustration of a nineteenth century industrial landscape. This is what many industrial towns used to look like

The most impressive factories are giant steelworks, oil refineries and shipyards. But far more people work in thousands of smaller factories and works scattered around towns and cities. Some of these can be very large, such as car factories, or they can be small and employ only a dozen or so workers.

Let us look at the ways of finding out, or at least guessing, why a factory is in one part of a town rather than another. Whatever its size, a factory is where raw materials are brought together and made into something different. Machinery and equipment are usually used, and a large building and piece of land is needed for this. Men and women are needed to do the work, even though nowadays much is automated and controlled by computers. So a factory needs to be fairly easily reached by the workforce. One reason why new factories are often found quite far from the centre of cities is because motor transport is more readily available to most workers than it used to be.

Some factories and workshops are in the city centre, often mixed in among shops and offices or older housing. This is partly because the city centre was where manufacturing began, but also because some products such as clothing and furniture are sold or used there. But this central land is needed for other purposes. Many of these small workshops and factories have been closed down because they could not make a profit in these places, or knocked down as the area has been redeveloped. They have usually been replaced by offices and shops.

When a river or stream flows through a town you will almost certainly find industries along its banks unless it is a very attractive riverside walk conserved for recreation or tourism. At the big ports there will obviously be riverside factories, but even in inland towns factories line the river banks. This is often because in the past the rivers were used by barges carrying raw materials or finished products. The factories stay there even if barges can no longer use the river. Nowadays new factories are more likely to be attracted to roads and railways.

Scattered in the suburbs, usually on industrial estates, are the factories that need more space and fairly flat land. Some of these are giant works making things such as cigarettes, cars or chemicals. Others are the more noisy, dangerous smelly factories that have to be kept away from houses. It is not surprising that houses near factories are usually cheaper than the average. Finally, scattered throughout the town are factories producing high value, small items that are used throughout the country, such as electronics works. These are often attractive buildings in pleasant settings.

1 What are the difficulties of running a small workshop or factory in the city centre or the old inner city housing area?
2 Why do so many factory owners site their works on the banks of rivers and canals, or alongside railway lines and main roads?
3 Compare this old picture of a Victorian industrial area with the estate at Telford shown on page 25.
4 What sort of factories or works are A, B, C, and D likely to be?

An example of an industrial building from the 1930s

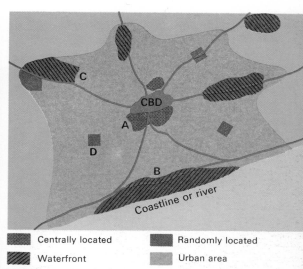

A model map to show the location of different sorts of factory

Centrally located	Randomly located
Waterfront	Urban area
Suburban	

Left: A medium-sized factory. The bluish shape in the bottom left hand corner is the wing of the aeroplane from which the photograph was taken. What seem to be the advantages of this site for a factory?

69

Offices

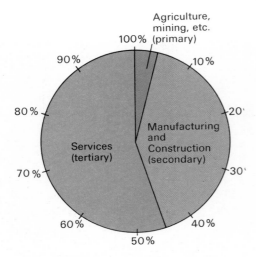

The proportion of people in jobs in the three main 'sectors' of work in Britain

Below: Office workers crossing from London Bridge Station to the City

Many people work in offices. They are not producing food or raw materials like farmers or miners, nor making things like factory workers. They will be keeping records, providing services for people, arranging holidays, loans for buying houses or the buying and selling of goods. They include what are sometimes called professional people such as solicitors, architects, managers and bankers, together with all their secretaries and assistants. Along with shop keepers and assistants, teachers, doctors, journalists, entertainers, bus, lorry and train drivers and many others their job is to make work and leisure run more smoothly and be more enjoyable. Quite a lot of people in Britain belong to this third or 'tertiary' group of workers.

Offices may be small with one or two people working in one room. On the other hand some offices are enormous employing thousands of people. Some buildings are used by many different companies, and their names will be shown at the entrance. If the whole of a building is owned or rented by one company then its name will probably be

Right: An imaginary advertisement for a new office building. Thousands of people will work in a modern purpose-built office block like this

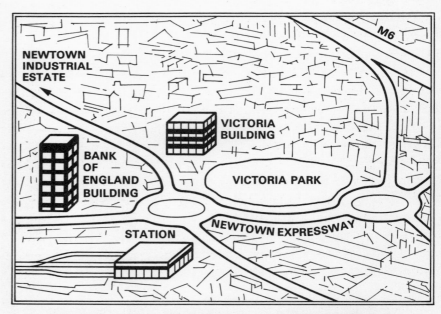

THE VICTORIA BUILDING

- Overlooking city centre
- Adjoining Newtown Expressway
- Fully air conditioned
- Double glazing
- Parking for 250 cars

Inside the drawing office at Ford motor works

Inside the reception area of a modern office building

clearly displayed. In other cases it is difficult to recognise that a building contains offices. It may be an old detached house or a terrace of houses used as family homes in the past. As office space gets short, the houses are converted into offices.

Offices are usually found in the same area as shops and banks. As with shops the smaller offices are widely scattered with the bigger ones in the more expensive central area. Because land is expensive the offices are often in tower blocks which suit them because they don't have to carry the massive machinery found in factories. The city centre is a good place for a large office. It is the easiest place for office workers to gather together from over a wide area, and it is convenient for all the big offices to be clustered together for business reasons. Even so, rates and rents are high. For this reason and because travelling into the centre of the city is getting difficult and expensive some offices have been moved out to the outskirts of the city or into another part of the country altogether.

1   What percentage of workers were there in the tertiary sector – this includes all those doing office jobs – in Britain in the 1970s?
2   Give the names of a bank, building society, travel agent, insurance company, and solicitor that has an office near your school or home. Are they in converted or purpose-built buildings?
3   Five reasons are given to attract firms to offices in the centre of 'Newtown'. Write a sentence explaining why each is desirable.
4   Name and describe the location of an office near your home or school that does work for **a**) the local authority **b**) the government. What general name is given to people who work for local or central government?

Sport for all

Children's play area in a park in the city

Right, below: Older men playing bowls

Football in the local park

People of all ages can be found taking part in some form of sport or exercise. Walking, jogging or joining a physical education class are good ways of keeping healthy and fit. Many people, though, enjoy taking part in some sort of sport. As well as keeping them fit, there is the enjoyment of using various skills and the excitement of competing against other people or teams. Older people, who cannot take part in very active sports against younger ones, stop playing games like rugby or football and spend more time on activities such as swimming or bowls or golf.

Most sports require special areas or buildings, like a football or cricket pitch, tennis courts, swimming pool and changing rooms. They are often expensive to build and look after. They are also big users of space. This is one reason why sports grounds are rare in the centres of cities and more common in the suburbs and outskirts of towns. On the other hand it is no good having play areas for children, football pitches or sports centres where nobody can get to them. They need to be accessible to people. Not only do they need to be easy to get to, they also need to be cheap enough for people to be able to afford to use them. Some of the cheapest grounds and centres are those owned by local authorities.

Small children, especially those who live in flats or homes without gardens, need somewhere to play. They usually like swings, climbing frames, sand pits and somewhere to run around and make a noise. These are often found in parks, and the children are taken there by their mothers, so they need to be near where the families live. There need to be a lot of these small play areas for young children scattered around housing areas.

Tennis courts and football pitches may be in local parks or on commons anywhere in the city, but the big areas of playing fields are most often in the suburbs. Golf courses are also likely to be on the outskirts of the town where there is more space and land values are lower. Swimming pools and sports centres can be found throughout the city, but they are usually located on bus or train routes or have car parks close at hand.

Sports Centre: a volleyball game in progress

1   Imagine you were responsible for sport and recreation in your town. What two sports would you provide for **a**) children under 10 years, **b**) young people between the ages of 10 and 18, **c**) people between the ages of 18–30, **d**) people between the ages of 30 and 60 **e**) elderly people over 60 years? You can mention the same sport and its facilities for more than one age group if you wish.

2   What are the differences between the small play area and the large sports centre? Consider the following: what is provided, number within the town, how people get there, who uses it, where it is likely to be, cost.

3   What are the reasons for and against the general public being allowed to use sports grounds and swimming pools belonging to schools in the area?

4   Put into words how Leeds is provided with open space and parks. Try to explain why it is like this.

Inside a swimming pool. People of all ages enjoy swimming

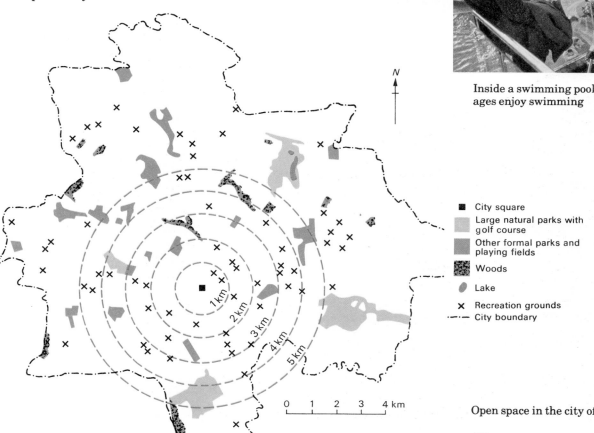

■ City square

▨ Large natural parks with golf course

▦ Other formal parks and playing fields

▨ Woods

◖ Lake

✕ Recreation grounds

–··– City boundary

0   1   2   3   4 km

Open space in the city of Leeds

Entertainment

Afternoon Bingo in the suburbs

Right: First Division football: big entertainment

First Division football clubs, 1981

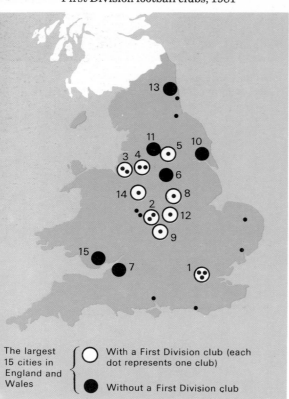

The largest 15 cities in England and Wales

○ With a First Division club (each dot represents one club)

● Without a First Division club

Some of the most popular sorts of entertainment, such as watching TV, playing records or reading, take place at home. Many people, though, enjoy going out for their entertainment.

This might mean going down the road to a local club or pub to meet friends. There you might have a drink, go to a disco, share some hobby or take part in some event. On the other hand it might mean making a longer journey to a different part of town to visit a theatre, cinema, sports ground or park, for a special occasion. This might be a fairly regular trip to see the local football team or a once-a-year trip to a theatre to see a visiting pop group or to listen to a concert.

Some of these entertainments are free. Anyone can listen to a band playing in the park. But more often it costs something. The charge may be just to cover the expenses of putting on the event. But in many cases it is to make a profit. Entertainment can also be big business!

Entertainment often takes place in buildings designed for that purpose, such as a theatre. But they can take place in other buildings, such as an office building where you may find a small jazz club in the basement. Some entertainment centres are used for many different purposes, such as dances, plays, concerts and sporting events. These are often placed in huge buildings. Some of the biggest buildings and space users in our cities are for entertainment.

Pop concert

Covent Garden Opera House

Clubs and pubs and other small places for local users are scattered around housing areas and the suburbs, with the occasional cinema or theatre in the suburban centre. But the biggest indoor places of entertainment tend to be concentrated in the city centre. This is the only part of the centre that comes to life at night after all the offices and shops have closed. The biggest and best known entertainment area in Britain is the 'West End' of London, while most of the national centres for various sports are also in the capital.

1 What is the difference in the numbers and the location of public houses and theatres in your town or area? Why is this?
2 Make a list of any buildings you know that are used for the following types of leisure and entertainment, **a**) historic building attracting tourists, **b**) museum, **c**) concert hall or theatre, **d**) cinema, **e**) sports ground. Think of your own area and of famous places in different parts of the country
3 Which of the 15 biggest cities in England and Wales had a) more than one First Division football club, b) no First Division football club in 1981?
4 What are the following 'places of entertainment' known for? Put them into two separate groups based on their use. Wembley Stadium, Wimbledon, Covent Garden, Tower of London, Crystal Palace, National Gallery, Lords, Olympia, The London Palladium. Where are they all? What does this tell us about that city?

The West End of London at night. The 'Talk of the Town' restaurant and night club

Land use

Leicester: Central Business District

If you travel from the edge of a town to its centre you will notice many changes in the way the land is used. We have seen some of the ways land is used in the past few pages. These land uses are like the parts of a jig-saw, and when they are put together they make a pattern of land use for the whole town.

Some places are used almost entirely for homes such as flats, maisonettes, terraced, semi-detached and detached houses. They may be old or new, spaced out at a low density or packed together at high density. They may be privately owned or rented, cheap or expensive. Every town has a number of different sorts of residential area.

In most towns there will be factories or works strung out along a main road, railway line, river bank or canal, or on an industrial estate. There will almost certainly be parks, commons and open space for recreation and leisure. In some places will be the buildings providing services to keep the town running – gas works and power stations, waste disposal and sewage works, telephone exchanges and bus or railway stations.

Dotted around will be clusters of shops and offices, but the biggest cluster of tall office blocks, big shops and stores, hotels and theatres will be in the Central Business District at the heart of the town.

Old inner city housing near the centre of Leicester (*above*) and a new high-rise development nearby (*right*)

76

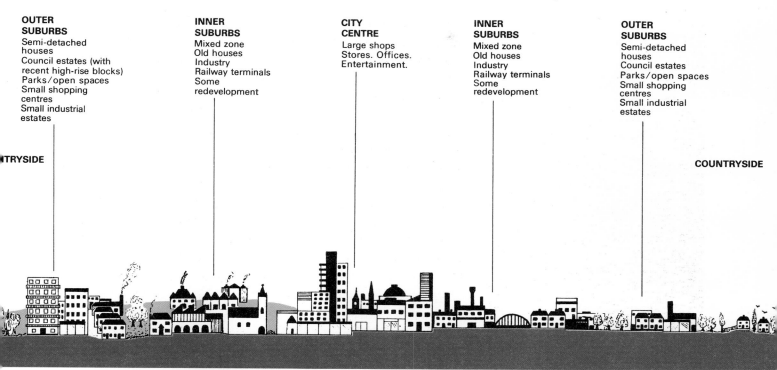

A town profile

OUTER SUBURBS
Semi-detached houses
Council estates (with recent high-rise blocks)
Parks/open spaces
Small shopping centres
Small industrial estates

INNER SUBURBS
Mixed zone
Old houses
Industry
Railway terminals
Some redevelopment

CITY CENTRE
Large shops
Stores. Offices.
Entertainment.

INNER SUBURBS
Mixed zone
Old houses
Industry
Railway terminals
Some redevelopment

OUTER SUBURBS
Semi-detached houses
Council estates
Parks/open spaces
Small shopping centres
Small industrial estates

COUNTRYSIDE

COUNTRYSIDE

The pattern of land use is not the result of pure chance or accident – too many towns look very much the same for that to be the case. We have seen why it makes sense for the main business activity to be in the city centre, for example, and why factories are in some places but not others. The diagram and map show imaginary towns, but many real ones are quite like them. We should remember two things. The boundaries between the different land uses are rarely sharp – one sort merges into the next. The land use in any part of the town is also likely to change as old buildings are knocked down and new ones put up or roads built. The land use of a town will also be affected by its site – where there is high ground, for example, you will be likely to find the residential area.

1 Copy the map of the imaginary town on page 69 and say what sort of land use you would expect at A, B, C, and D.
2 Why are so many of the buildings in the central area – shops and offices, for example – 'high-rise' or very tall?
3 Suggest several reasons why there is far less 'high-rise' building in the suburbs and outer edge of the city than in the centre.
4 Imagine a walk through your town or one that you know well. Name one place for each of the land uses mentioned in the description or shown in the photographs.

A well-established suburban road in Leicester

Routes

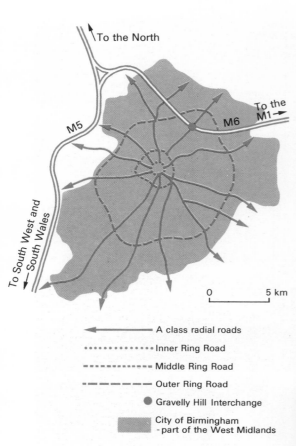

To the M1 →

M5

M6

To South West and South Wales

0   5 km

⟵⟶ A class radial roads

·········· Inner Ring Road

---------- Middle Ring Road

— — — — Outer Ring Road

● Gravelly Hill Interchange

City of Birmingham - part of the West Midlands

The pattern of roads in Birmingham. Main radial and ringway routes

Right: Transport routes and terminals are big users of land. The Paddington area of London

People and goods have to move in towns. If the transport system of a town broke down completely there would be chaos, and ordinary daily life would be impossible. We get some idea of how difficult things would be when there is very severe weather or a transport strike.

Movements take place along 'routes' such as footways, roads, railways and canals. These routes take up a lot of space in towns. When seen from above they make lines or linear patterns, sometimes called 'networks'. The points where routes cross or end are called 'nodes'. Road junctions or railway terminals are examples of nodes. If shown on a map, they too would make a pattern. They would make a dot pattern, though, not a linear one.

Line patterns made by streets differ a great deal. In the old parts of a town the pattern is usually twisting and turning, quite unlike the regular straight lines of inner city terraced housing or the gentle curves of the later semi-detached houses of the suburbs.

If we look at the pattern made by main roads we see that they often lead to the city centre like the spokes of a wheel. This is called a radial pattern. Because of the many road junctions with traffic lights it is usually a long and difficult journey to cross from one side to the other of a town. To make cross-town journeys easier dual carriage-

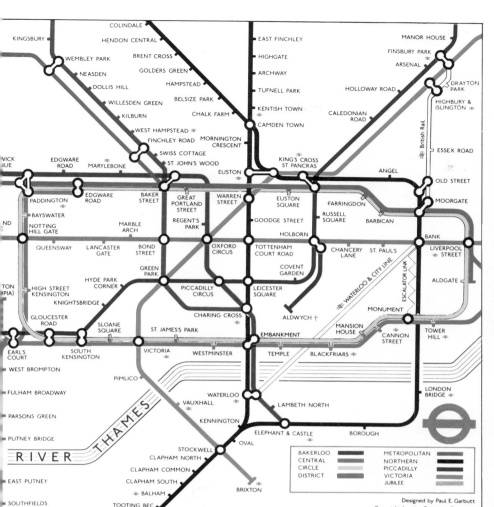

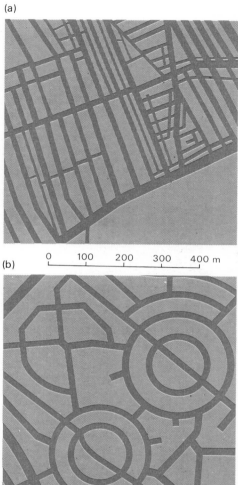

Street patterns in the city; (a) Victorian housing area and (b) inter-war council estate

ways or urban motorways have been built in circles or rings at varying distances from the city centre. Many towns have their 'inner' and 'outer' ringways.

Most towns have only one main railway line and railway station, but London has a number of terminals. The railway lines radiate from the capital to all parts of Britain. The main line terminals, and many other parts of the city, are linked by the network of the London Underground system. The map doesn't tell us the actual routes nor the true distances between stations. But on the underground we want to know which stations are next to which and where to change from one line to another. We can tell this from the underground map.

1   Trace or copy the street patterns from the maps on this page. Write down their differences in your own words. Measure the total length of roads within a 200 metre square on each map. This will give the density of the streets in each area.

2   What are the arguments for and against building 'ring roads' in towns?

3   What do you notice about the locations of the London railway terminals? Suggest why the terminals are in this pattern.

4   Describe how you would get from a) Paddington to Waterloo station, b) Southfields to Camden Town, by London Underground. Give two routes for the second journey, giving the difference in the number of stations and the number of changes to be made.

New Town

Cumbernauld New Town

Houses in a neighbourhood of Cumbernauld – with a few local residents!

One of the striking things about Cumbernauld is that all the buildings look fairly new. This is not really surprising since building only began in 1956. That may seem a long time ago, but compared with most of our towns it is very recent.

Cumbernauld is a New Town. It has been built (and is still being built) to provide homes and jobs for people from the overcrowded and older parts of Glasgow. One day about 70 000 people will live there.

Cumbernauld has been built on the top and sides of a low hill. The town centre is on the hilltop, and it takes about twenty minutes to walk from here to the further housing. The centre is very different from most High Streets. It is really one huge building. At ground level and below are the storage spaces and car parks for 500 cars. Shoppers can walk in traffic-free areas on the upper floors. The shops are laid out around open spaces and enclosed squares. As well as shops there are banks, offices, public houses, library, church and a swimming pool as well as a technical college.

In the residential areas the houses and flats are fairly close together. Even so, there is plenty of open space, and this has been landscaped with grass and trees. The main roads are away from the houses, schools and small neighbourhood shops.

There are almost thirty other New Towns in this country. They were built to provide jobs as well as houses. They were not meant to be commuter towns with people travelling elsewhere to work. As in other New Towns Cumbernauld Corporation has to attract firms to the town by building factories in advance, offering loans and giving other help. The factories are on several sites around the edge of the town. It is easy to get to the railway and roads that lead to Glasgow about 20 kilometres to the south-west, and to other parts of Scotland.

In old cities and towns many of the amenities have grown without planning and things that people like, such as the shape of a street or an interesting mixture of buildings, are often 'accidental'. In a New Town these unexpected but interesting townscapes are difficult to plan.

1   There are several different sorts of dwelling shown in the photographs. Choose one that you think you would enjoy living in and describe it and its surroundings. Use a sketch if you prefer, adding labels to show what you like about it.
2   Cars and lorries have been kept well away from pedestrians, but allowance has been made for car ownership. How is this shown by the photographs and description?
3   Describe the site, shape and location of Cumbernauld.
4   What sorts of industry would you expect to find on the industrial estates of Cumbernauld? Name three industries you would not expect to find.
5   Write a few words about why you would rather live in a New Town than where you live now. If you already live in a New Town, describe what you like and what you dislike about it.

New Towns and Cities in Britain

Walking home. The town centre is within easy reach in Cumbernauld

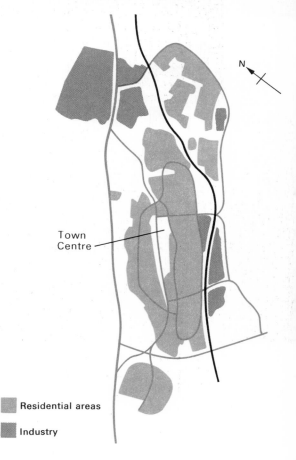

Land use in Cumbernauld

81

New City

Right: Part of the New City of Milton Keynes

A modern factory in Milton Keynes

Below: An advertisement to attract industry to Milton Keynes

Milton Keynes is another New Town. It is planned to become much bigger than Cumbernauld. When completed there should be about 250 000 people there, which is between three and four times as many. It should really be called a New City. It is hoped there will be over 130 000 jobs in new factories and offices, but that will depend on companies being attracted to the new city. It is placed far enough away from London to be attractive to people wanting to get away from the Capital City. But it is still in the south-east area where jobs are more plentiful than elsewhere.

Quite clearly one big city centre like the one at Cumbernauld will not be enough for all these people. There will be a number of other areas with shops and offices as well as the main one. Some of these will be placed in villages and small towns that already exist in this part of Buckinghamshire – Stony Stratford, Wolverton, Bletchley and Fenny Stratford are the main ones.

Each neighbourhood with its houses, shops, schools, offices and factories will be linked to others by a network of roads just as in any other city. In the case of Milton Keynes, though, they are nearly all newly built or being built. As the map shows they form a grid of squares and rectangles with slight curves and changes of direction here and there. Within this grid pattern of roads there will be many different sorts of land use. There will be housing areas, shopping centres, industrial estates, hospitals, the Open University, schools colleges, sewage disposal works, reservoirs and a lot of open space for recreation and sport.

Land use in Milton Keynes

Milton Keynes will have all the things that are needed in a city, but unlike our older ones it was planned as a whole from the beginning rather than growing over centuries. It will be interesting to see if it turns out to be a more enjoyable place to live in than our unplanned cities.

1 Describe the location of Milton Keynes in relation to London and Birmingham. What important transport routes will link it to these two very big cities?

2 How long would it take to drive from Stony Stratford to Fenny Stratford centres along a main road at an average speed of 50 km per hour, and to drive across Milton Keynes on the Motorway at 110 km per hour? How far is it from the middle of the city centre to the furthest boundary?

3 Look at the area east of the Grand Union Canal. Count the numbers of a) first schools, b) middle schools, c) secondary schools. Explain the difference in number and in their locations.

4 Look at the map of New Towns on page 81. Which New Towns seem to have been built to help provide homes and jobs for the people of London, Liverpool, Glasgow and Birmingham? Which of these would be better called a New City, like Milton Keynes?

The shopping area in Bletchley, Milton Keynes

Damage to the city

Old houses next to a factory: Deptford in London

Some parts of our towns and cities are pleasing to look at and enjoyable to live, work and relax in. But other parts are certainly not! Sometimes the ugliness and squalor is due to what happened in the past when many people were poorer and forced to expect less from their homes and surroundings than we do now. Many older areas, as we have seen, are crowded. The houses are mixed in with noisy, smelly or dangerous factories, and they often lack indoor amenities that we now have a right to expect such as hot water and baths. Even if the local authority responsible for building houses knocks them down to put up better homes, there may be years in which large patches of land are left ugly and derelict, and then more years of noisy building.

There are other changes that can affect people. Nobody wants to live in poor housing, but it may be better than nothing. It is hard for some people to see why houses should be replaced by new offices or car parks or motorways that may not be built for years, or even really needed. New roads and motorways may please car and lorry users who want to travel through the city as smoothly as possible, but may not seem so good to those who have to live near them.

Another obvious cause of damage to cities and to the lives of people who live in them is pollution of the air. This may be caused by dangerous fumes from factories or the exhaust fumes from cars and lorries. Noise is another sort of pollution that may be not only just a nuisance, but at times a real danger to health.

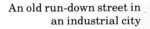

An old run-down street in an industrial city

Three examples of damage to the environment: a vandalized telephone box (*left*), domestic litter on wasteland (*centre*) and a young tree senselessly broken in half

One form of damage for which many ordinary individuals are responsible is the dropping of litter in streets or public places. Some of them also scribble graffitti or leave their junk in places used by other people. It costs a great deal of money to get rid of these eyesores and nuisances. This money has to be paid for from the rates and taxes and could be better spent on other things. Even more damaging is the vandalism caused to property used by the general public, such as telephone kiosks, public lavatories, lifts, escalators, parks and buildings. If you look around you will almost certainly see the unfortunate damage and ugliness caused by a mixture of bad planning, greed and selfishness.

1 Compare the photograph of the houses in Barnsbury with the one on the next page. What has happened?
2 Imagine you had vandalised the kiosk in the picture, or had dropped some of the litter. Write down a few of the thoughts going through your mind as you did it. Why do many people get angry about this sort of vandalism? Do you think it matters or not?
3 List some of the **a**) eyesores, **b**) nuisances, **c**) dangers in the environment around your home or school. Who has caused them? What could be done about them?
4 A patch of land in a town is wanted for different purposes – a business man wants to build offices on it; the council wants to build houses; a group of parents want it to be used as an adventure playground and shopkeepers want a car park for shoppers. Write down the arguments in favour of each idea, and the objections. Why is it sometimes difficult to decide the best use of the land?

Barnsbury Street in London. These twelve derelict houses were bought by the local council and were converted to thirty nine flats by a housing association with the help of the Council. The picture on the next page shows what they looked like after they were converted.

85

Planning for people

Right: The Barnsbury Street houses after conversion

The way planners would like to redevelop an older part of the inner city of Bristol (St. Paul's): an architect's plan (*bottom of page*), and an architect's drawing (*below*)

Many of the things that happen in towns and cities are the responsibility of the local council. The men and women who belong to the County Council (or Metropolitan County Council in the case of the big cities) look after some things such as roads and longer-term planning while the smaller District Councils look after things such as housing and rubbish collection. There may be five or six Districts in a County or Metropolitan County.

Men and women such as planners, highway engineers, and architects are employed by these local councils to do certain jobs. They advise the councillors and suggest what things might be done, but in the end the councillors make the decisions. The money for doing these jobs comes from the 'rates' that people who own property in the area pay, or from rents and other income, or from grants paid by the central government out of our taxes. So what happens depends partly on how much money there is and how councillors spend it.

People want all sorts of things to be done in the town, but there is rarely enough money or land for everything. Planners and councillors on the planning committees have to decide what developments they

Wall paintings can brighten up a fairly drab and uninteresting bit of the town: Queen's Crescent, London

Children from the St Paul's area taking part in a planning exercise in the classroom

The 'Keep Britain Tidy' group is one of many voluntary groups that tries to keep the town pleasant to live in

will allow. They have to decide whether to give permission for such things as building an extension on your house or putting up a new factory or a new housing estate. In this way it is hoped to control ugly or dangerous developments. Other planners try to decide what should happen to the area in the future to satisfy people's needs for homes, work, schools and recreation. Some plans may cover the whole county and others just a few buildings in a street. At the same time as deciding 'what' should be done, planners also have to decide 'where' things should go. They have to decide in favour of one of a number of competing claims for space.

Everybody has the right to join in discussions on these plans, as well as to elect the councillors that make the decisions. On the whole, people only get involved when something is going to happen that will affect them fairly soon. One example may be to build a new road or factory near their house. Apart from this though there are many other ways for individuals or voluntary groups to involve themselves in their area. They can paint walls, help to clear derelict sites, plant trees, avoid dropping litter or rubbish, and persuade councillors to spend some money on making the town a pleasant place to live in.

1   What is the name of a) your District Council, b) your Metropolitan or County Council? Name one thing for which each is responsible in your area, and one thing that each has done to change the environment.
2   What are the names of a) your District Chief Planner and Chairman of the Planning Committee, b) your County Chief Planner and Chairman of the County Planning Committee? Where are your District and County Planning Offices?
3   What are some of the jobs done by a planner, an architect, a highways engineer and a parks superintendent?
4   What are some of the advantages and disadvantages of your having to get permission to build something in an area?
5   Name some of the voluntary groups in your town that try to influence or improve the local environment. Describe any jobs that you or your friends have done to help tidy up or improve the local area.

Daily journeys to work

Right: London commuters at Liverpool Street station, London

Evening rush hour in the heart of London

A simple time-distance map of three journeys

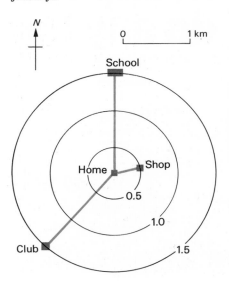

Most of us spend a lot of time moving from one place to another. We make these journeys for all sorts of reasons. During the week some member of the family is likely to be going to work or to school. At week ends or during holidays longer journeys may be taken. Some long journeys may be fairly regular, such as going to the nearest football ground to watch a football match. On the other hand it might be a special visit to the country or seaside or to see relatives.

As well as being of different lengths and times, journeys can be made in many different ways. For shorter journeys we walk or cycle, but for all but the shortest journeys we usually take a bus or train or go by car. Longer journeys can be done by plane. It is simple to fly from London to Glasgow and back in a day, for example. But this costs a lot, and no one is likely to travel this far to work each day. Most daily journeys to work are made by road or rail. Very often two or three different methods of travel are used on a single journey. Lots of commuters drive from home to the local station, take a train to the centre of the city and then go by bus or underground train to their place of work.

Because many jobs start and end at about the same time, there are many people wanting to travel at the same time. This means that buses and trains get packed with people and streets crowded with traffic. These 'rush hours' happen twice a day, as people arrive at and leave offices, shops, factories and other workplaces. The number of people in a city travelling to work each day can be enormous. London

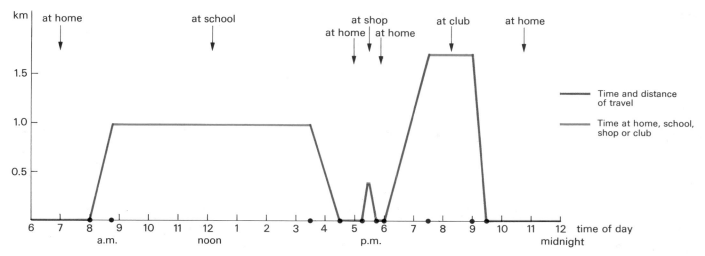

A time-distance diagram of three journeys

Transport, for example, carries over six million people on every week day, and most of these people are travelling to and from work. This is more than the populations of Birmingham, Manchester, Glasgow and Liverpool put together. It is no wonder that rush hours in London are frantic times, and that the slightest delay or breakdown causes chaos.

1 Look at the diagram showing the three journeys made on one day by a pupil. Give reasons for these, and say how long each one took. What was the distance travelled from home to the three destinations?

2 Say why you think it took longer to travel to the club than to get back? (there are several possible reasons).

3 What are the advantages and disadvantages of the map over the diagram for describing the three journeys?

4 Imagine you are one of the people in one of the photographs. Describe your feelings and what you are likely to be thinking about the journey.

Car workers cycling to their factory

Maps of journeys

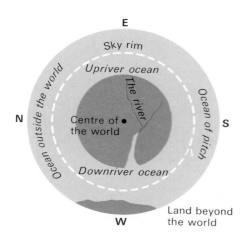

The 'mental map' of the world of the Yurok Indians of Northern California

Before the White Man came this small tribe thought that the world was 150 miles wide and that the river on which they lived was its centre

The journeys we make follow certain 'routes', and these can be shown on a map. In the example shown below a pupil has painted a map from memory of the route taken from home to school. Everybody has a 'memory map' or 'mental map' of the journeys they make, although they may not be very clear or accurate! This may be because we have only travelled along the route once or twice, but most of us even have inaccurate memory maps of journeys we have made many times. This is partly because we do not look very carefully as we travel, and only remember buildings or open spaces or signs that remind us which direction to take. We only remember the things that catch our eye because they are unusual or because they interest us or because we need to spot them in order to take the right direction. The rest we don't bother to 'see'.

By the side of the other example of a memory map is a map that is true to scale – things are in the correct places next to each other. By using the scale we can measure quite accurately the distance between places. This map tells us the routes followed by the pupil who did the second memory map and two other pupils as well. From the key we can see what methods they used to make these journeys. It would be interesting to know how long each journey took – the one by car took less time than the one on foot, even though the distance was greater.

A 'memory map' or 'mental map' drawn by a pupil of the route taken from home to school. Westminster Abbey appears in the bottom right-hand corner

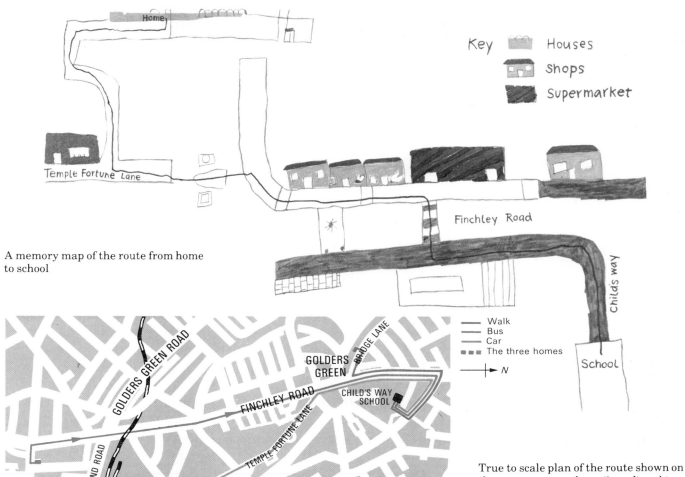

A memory map of the route from home to school

True to scale plan of the route shown on the memory map above (in red) and two other routes by bus and car (in blue and green)

Since the journey to school by bus was made during the rush hour it took far longer than it would have done at other times.

The maps do not tell us how much traffic flowed along the routes – how busy the roads were. There may be twenty or thirty buses going along the road between eight and nine o'clock in the morning but only a few in the afternoon between two and three o'clock. There is a simple way of showing how many people or how much traffic 'flows' along a route in a given time. The density of the flow is shown by the thickness of the line – the thicker the line the more traffic or people.

1 The pupil at the school illustrated on page 90 travels from the house in the top left of the map or picture to the school near the bottom. What seem to be the interesting or important things along this route? What are the good and poor things about this map?

2 What seem to be the most important parts of the journey made by the school pupil above? Measure the actual distances from home to school of the three journeys

3 Copy the three routes from the map. Imagine that two pupils walked the one route, four travelled in the car and ten used the bus. Draw a flow map to show these facts. Make sure you add a key.

4 Draw a map of your own route to school. You may either choose to draw an 'accurate' true to scale map, or a more imaginative 'mental' map.

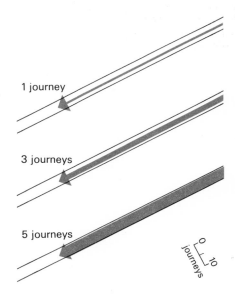

How to show the number of people or the amount of traffic flowing along a route. The thicker the line the greater the density of people or traffic

Longer and less regular journeys

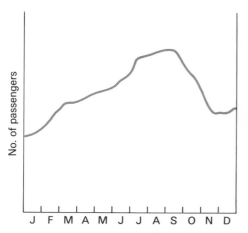

Passenger movement at Heathrow Airport throughout a year. When is it greatest? Why then?

Right, below: Supporters approaching the ground near the beginning of a match

Holiday passengers at an airport

Although by far the most journeys each year are made by people going to and from work, there are many other reasons why people travel from place to place.

There are the fairly short journeys made to local shops or to see friends once or twice a week. Other local journeys to places such as a library or club or doctor's surgery may be made less often. We are willing to travel further for special events that happen only once or twice a year. These journeys usually take longer and cost more than local ones. Examples of these include going to concerts or sporting events in a nearby big town, or visiting relatives for a few days in a distant part of the country. We don't mind spending a fair amount of time or money on these special journeys.

Just as there are rush hours when a lot of people want to get to and from work all at the same time, so there are crowds and dense traffic just before and after special events that attract large numbers of people. Movement is often difficult near a theatre or playing field at the end of an event when everyone wants to get away as soon as possible.

Anyone who has gone to a beauty spot in the countryside or the seaside on a summer week-end or a Bank Holiday will know that the traffic builds up at certain times of the morning and evening just as it does during the 'rush hour'. The roads out of the town are full as

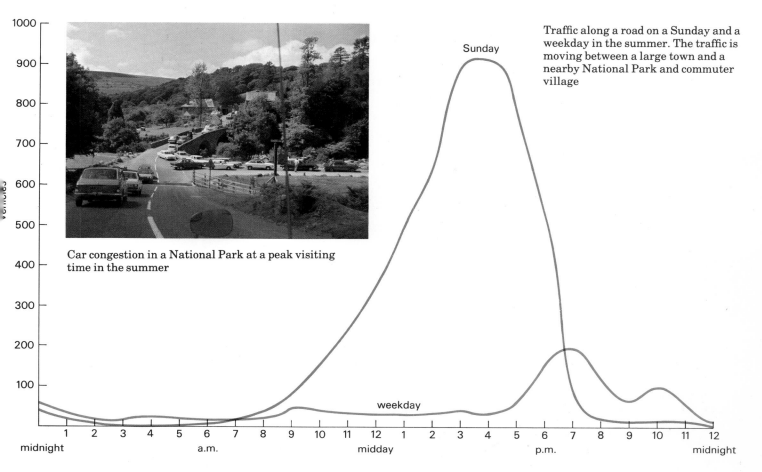

Traffic along a road on a Sunday and a weekday in the summer. The traffic is moving between a large town and a nearby National Park and commuter village

Car congestion in a National Park at a peak visiting time in the summer

people leave in the morning and in the evening as they make their way home. As the photograph shows, at certain times of the day the traffic flow may be very dense in one direction and very light in the other. Traffic may be forced to go very slowly and there may be a traffic jam of many kilometres.

The scene at the airport reminds us that many people take their holidays at the same time of the year, usually in summer. There are certain times when holiday traffic is very heavy, and this shows particularly clearly at airports and seaports where there may be great crowds of holiday passengers waiting for aircraft or ships, or others just arriving from holidays overseas. Just as there are daily rush hours, there are also seasons when there is a great deal of movement.

1   How often do you or your family make a journey to **a**) a grocers shop, **b**) a school, **c**) a sporting event, **d**) a concert, **e**) a week-long holiday **f**) see relatives at Christmas? How long are these journeys, on average?
2   Look at the graph of traffic flows along a road on two different days. What is the difference between the number of cars using the road on Sundays and on the weekday? How does the traffic flow throughout the day differ between the weekday and the Sunday?
3   When is traffic likely to be greatest leaving **a**) a Football League week-end match, **b**) a Football League mid-week match, **c**) a matinee performance at a theatre, **d**) an evening performance at a theatre?
4   Find out when members of the class go on an annual holiday (if they do so!). Which is the most popular month? Draw a graph to show this, and give a suitable title.

One-way traffic congestion on the M5 Motorway. Most people are heading for seaside resorts in Avon and North Somerset or holidays in Devon and Cornwall

Inter-city rail

Inter-City 125. This picture shows how comfortable the interior of a railway carriage can be

Right, above: An Inter-City 125 diesel-driven passenger train making easy going of the snow

Differences in passenger travel between 1955 and 1975

	Changes in use of different means of transport (expressed as a percentage)		Increase or decrease in use from 1955 to 1975
	1955	1975	
Airways	0.15%	0.55%	+ 366%
Railways	18.50%	8.15%	− 227%
Roads: public transport	39.00%	12.20%	− 320%
Roads: private transport	42.35%	79.10%	+ 187%
	100.00%	100.00%	

The painting on page 100 shows what the earliest trains looked like. These engines were driven by steam, and the heat provided by burning coal. The first railway to use steam-driven locomotives was the Stockton to Darlington line, which opened in 1825. For the next eighty to ninety years a number of different railway companies laid down thousands of kilometres of track throughout Britain along with the tunnels, cuttings, embankments and bridges that contained and carried the track. All towns of any size had a railway station, and even in the countryside few places were more than an hour by horse and carriage from one.

Many changes have happened to the railways since then. The greatest total length of railway track existed in about 1914. Since then almost half the lines have been closed down and often completely removed, along with signalling equipment and railway stations. This has been partly due to competition from road transport for travel over shorter journeys and in the countryside and air transport for longer journeys. Most of the rail closures have been in rural areas, and bigger towns are still linked by rail.

Nowadays the vast majority of rail passengers are carried on Inter-City trains or on suburban commuter trains that link big cities with the surrounding smaller towns. All the original companies have been nationalised (taken over by the State) to become British Rail. There are a few private lines left using steam locomotives on short stretches of track for recreation or tourist purposes. Today, all trains are either diesel or electric powered. The Advanced Passenger Train, due to be widely used in the 1980s, will reach speeds of over 200 km per hour. Apart from the locomotives the carriages and rolling stock are also designed for these high speeds, while the signalling system is now largely automatic to be as safe as possible. Inter-City services are trying hard to win back passengers from road and air transport.

1 Draw a bar graph to show the information about passenger traffic given in the table.
2 What are some of the advantages of rail over other sorts of passenger travel? Is rail likely to be best for **a**) short, **b**) medium or **c**) long journeys? What are some of the disadvantages of rail travel?
3 Copy the time chart. Add lines to represent travel times to Swansea, Norwich and Liverpool.
4 The map tell us some things about Inter-City routes, but not other things. What does the map tell us? What are we not told or helped to discover? Look again at the Underground map on page 79. What is the most important thing about these 'topological' maps?

Electric-powered passenger train

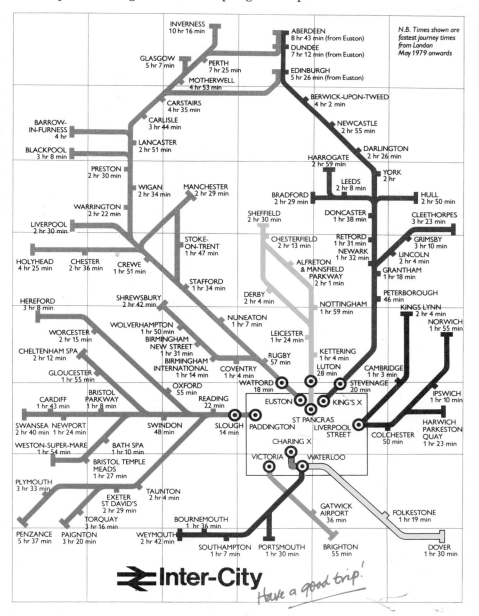

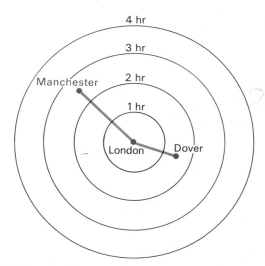

Time chart from London to a number of cities using the Inter-City services

Left: Inter-City 'Overground' map, with times of journeys added

95

Transport of goods

Juggernaut lorries are a cheap way to carry goods, but can cause a lot of noise, pollution and damage

Right: Lorries being unloaded in a container park

An advertisement for Speedlink, British Rail's computerised goods transport system

In addition to millions of passengers, vast amounts of goods are being moved around the country on most days of the year. Many of these goods may be big and bulky such as coal, iron ore, road gravel and steel girders. It is cheapest to carry these in large, specially designed lorries, railway wagons or ships, and to load and unload them with special equipment. This cuts down the cost of fuel and of loading and unloading. The bigger the lorry, wagon or ship, the cheaper the cost of transport.

Liquids and gases such as milk, petrol, water, natural gas and some chemicals are moved along pipelines. They are also sometimes carried in special containers driven by lorries. Special lorries and wagons have also been designed to carry frozen goods and dangerous chemicals such as nuclear waste.

Apart from these large and sometimes dangerous items there are huge quantities of smaller articles and packages to be moved. Many are carried by lorries and vans owned by private companies, or by the Post Office or British Rail. In recent years there has been a far greater use of containers for moving general goods. All sorts of items are packed inside the container and these are then carried by lorry, train or ship until they reach their destination. Dotted around the country are the big container-handling yards. Those are usually found near

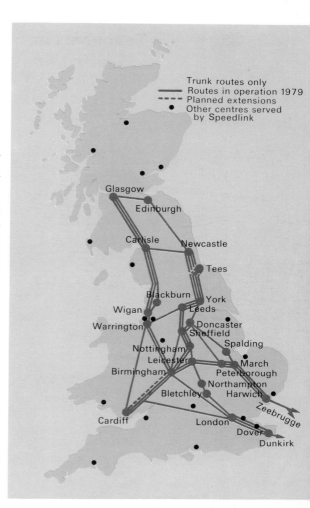

railway junctions or ports. Here the massive cranes load the containers from one type of transport to another without the parcels and packages and crates needing to be handled at all.

This method is not all that suitable for sending single small items from one place to another – it would be wasteful to have only one or two packages in a large container! British Rail are now providing a means of transporting smaller amounts of goods quickly from place to place with its computer-controlled Speedlink service.

1 What big advantages do lorries have over the railways for transporting goods? What are the advantages of rail over road?
2 Why would it be unusual to find **a**) steel girders carried by air, **b**) fresh-cut flowers sent by container lorry **c**) a single expensive watch sent by freightliner train?
3 What does the advertisement claim are the advantages of Speedlink? Look at the Speedlink map. Which city has most routes leading to it? Why are there few routes in Central and North Wales and North Scotland? Why are the fairly small towns of Harwich and Dover so important?
4 What are the advantages and disadvantages of transporting liquids or gases by pipeline rather than in some other way?
5 Make a list of the different kinds of liquids you have seen being carried in lorries.

A journey by container

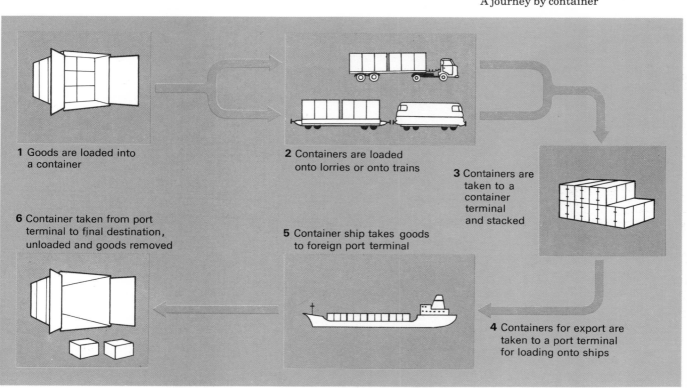

1 Goods are loaded into a container

2 Containers are loaded onto lorries or onto trains

3 Containers are taken to a container terminal and stacked

4 Containers for export are taken to a port terminal for loading onto ships

5 Container ship takes goods to foreign port terminal

6 Container taken from port terminal to final destination, unloaded and goods removed

Different needs and different means

Before any person takes a journey or sends something from one place to another, he has to decide on the best means of transport.

The things he has to take into account when travelling himself may include how much time can be afforded, how much money can be spent, whether there is a car available or a railway or bus station nearby and how much luggage will be taken. Some people get sick when travelling far by road, or by sea. (Perhaps you can think of other things). When all these have been taken into account a decision on the most suitable method of travelling can be made.

We have seen that bulky goods are best transported in large carriers by road, rail or sea, and that to save costs of handling it is often a good idea to carry things in containers. But one problem of using large lorries, wagons or ships is that they are fairly slow, while the big 'juggernaut' lorries can do damage to the environment. So the gains in cost have to be balanced against slow journey times and possible nuisance or damage. Quite a lot of bulky goods are carried on river and canal barges in some parts of the country.

For door-to-door convenience, cars, vans and lorries are probably the best means of transport. For middle distance travel rail combines speed and comfort (for people), but there is need to get to and from the stations. Air travel is fast, but usually fairly expensive, and there is

Above: A scene at Gatwick Airport. How many different kinds of transport can you see?

Right: Laying a pipeline through the countryside

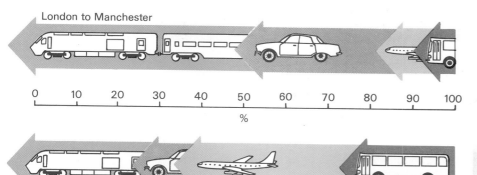

London to Manchester

0 10 20 30 40 50 60 70 80 90 100
%

London to Glasgow

Differences in journeys: London to Glasgow and London to Manchester

the same problem of getting to and from the airports. Flying time may be short, but the total journey quite long. Valuable cargo can also be carried by air if it is small and light, but not if it is heavy and bulky. If you live in a remote and distant place, such as an offshore island in the Orkneys or Shetlands, then smaller aircraft and helicopters are often the only means of transport.

1 Look at the diagram and the maps on pages 95 and 101. How far is it from London to Manchester and to Glasgow? What is the time of the fastest journey to both? Explain the differences in distance and travel times?

2 Why do you think a greater proportion of people a) fly from London to Glasgow than London to Manchester, b) go by car from London to Manchester than London to Glasgow.

3 Why have Inverness, Paris and New York 'shrunk' on the time map compared to a true distance map? Why has the Isle of Wight and the town of Shanklin 'moved' further away than it is on a true distance map?

4 How many different forms of transport can be seen on these two pages? Make a list of them all and give one good and one bad thing about each.

Barges carrying coal to a power station

A 'time-of-travel' map based on London

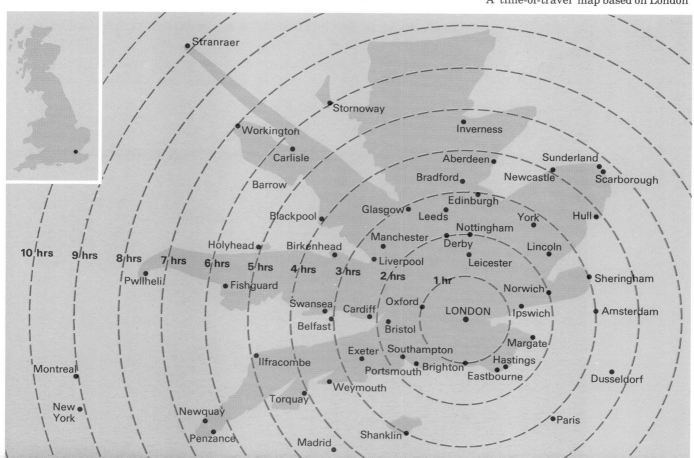

New landscapes

The Liverpool and Manchester Railway
1831. First Class and Mail (*above*) and
Second and Third Class passenger
carriages (*below*)

In early times, whenever a route was used again and again some sort
of track became marked over the landscape. When the route reached a
river that was too deep to be forded, a bridge had to be built. The
trouble was that these paths and tracks became either very muddy or
very dusty depending on the weather. The first people to make roads
suitable for use in all conditions were the Romans who did so by
giving them a hard surface of cobbles or stones. We have seen that one
of the things the Romans did was to build a number of long, straight
roads across Britain linking up their garrison towns. Much later on
methods were developed of building roads with tarmac and concrete.

A few hundred years ago when the roads were still very poor,
people began to dig canals in order to carry heavy, bulky goods. They
cut through hilly areas by means of tunnels and locks and crossed

Viaducts and aqueducts
built to carry railways
and canals across valleys
are a reminder of the
marvellous skills of the
early railway and canal
builders

valleys on magnificent aqueducts. Later on the railways replaced canals as the main method of transport. A burst of activity led to a network of railway tracks with their tunnels, cuttings, embankments, viaducts and bridges linking up most towns. There are plenty of reminders of these early routes and terminals still to be seen today.

In the last thirty or so years the most striking change to our environment has been due to a great increase in road transport. During this time the motorway system of roads has been built. The six-lane highways make a big impact on the countryside and the towns they pass through, while their junctions take up enormous areas of land.

Airports are also great land-users, especially the international ones such as Gatwick and Heathrow. Much of the land could be used for farming, and this is just one of the reasons why people are concerned about the building of a third airport near London.

Above: The motorways have made a new landscape that would have amazed our great-grandparents

Left above: The Severn Bridge carrying road traffic between England and Wales

The motorway network and bridges and tunnels crossing big estuaries

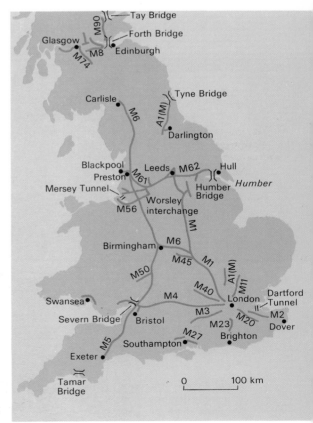

1   Choose a photograph from this book showing some form of transport route. Draw a sketch or write a description or poem saying how the environment has been changed.
2   Draw an imaginary map of a stretch of land with a road, railway or canal passing through it. With the help of the key on page 107, add various symbols to show as many things such as cuttings, embankments, aqueducts, bridges, tunnels and so on as you can.
3   From your atlas **a**) find the major estuaries of the United Kingdom ('estuary' means the mouth of a large river). Name the towns and cities shown next to the important tunnels and bridges crossing those big estuaries, **b**) name the cities on the motorway routes.
4   Work out the distances between Bristol and Cardiff and Grimsby and Hull before and after building the Severn and Humber bridges. What are the arguments for and against building big bridges like these? How are they paid for?

101

Eyesores, damage and pollution

'Smash the next lamp on the left, flatten the pavement by the pub, nudge the sweetshop, scrape the Market Cross, then just follow the skid marks to London'

Our lives would be very different without modern methods of travel and transport. Most of us would miss being able to travel some distance in order to work or visit friends or go on holidays. Most of us would also be a lot poorer without the wealth that lorries, trains, cars, ships and aeroplanes help to create. But we have to pay for this movement and wealth.

People who live near some roads have to put up with a stream of traffic, day and night. The constant movement and noise, as well as pollution from exhaust fumes can make people tired, miserable and at times unwell. The big 'juggernauts' that are used nowadays can do considerable damage as they rumble through the narrow, twisting roads of old town centres. Another problem is caused by the need to park cars and lorries. Land needed for other uses has to be given over to car parking in towns, while many residents have to put up with big lorries parked overnight in their streets.

The noise made by aircraft on take-off and landing can be a terrible nuisance to millions of people who are unfortunate enough to live near the main flight paths of any airport. The view of the plane opposite is a common one for such people. This is another reason why large numbers of residents in several places around London have joined together to protest about the building of another airport near their homes.

Traffic jam on the M4 exit at Chiswick

Right: People protesting against a scheme to demolish houses to make way for a new road

Although we may soon get used to it, there is also the question of the eyesore caused by such things as advertisements, road signs and directions, traffic signals and crossing signals. Because some signs are necessary and they do no actual harm, we tend to accept them. But they often do make a place more of a clutter and less pleasant to live in, and a little care and thought could avoid it.

We all benefit in some way or other from efficient transport, but there is a price to pay for it. One trouble is that those who suffer most directly (such as people living near an airport) are often not the ones enjoying the benefits.

1 Choose two of the illustrations on these pages and for each list the different sorts of 'eyesores, damage and pollution' they illustrate.
2 Imagine your feelings about the aircraft noise if you were **a**) living in the house beneath the flight path of the aeroplane, **b**) a passenger in the aeroplane. What might your thoughts and feelings be in each case? How are they likely to differ?
3 Look around your local streets. Draw or write about 'the ugliest and most confusing collection of traffic signs and controls in my area'. Can you think of ways these might be tidied up without taking away the information and instructions they give?
4 One of the most dangerous results of road traffic has not been mentioned so far. Can you think what this is, and how the danger might be reduced?

Imagine what it is like to live in a house like this near a major airport!

Advertisements (*left below*) and traffic signs (*below*) can dominate their surroundings

103

Moving home in Britain

House for sale, Corby. As the steel industry declines, people have to move elsewhere for work

A country cottage for sale. The new owner is likely to use it as a second home

The ages when people leave home

Almost all young people of fifteen years of age live at home. During the following ten years most of them leave their families. When they leave some move into houses or flats while others live in college or university buildings. Most, though, stay with their parents until they get married. They then move into their own home, if they are lucky enough to be able to rent or buy one!

Sometimes whole families move. They may do so because the mother or father has the chance of a better job or of earning more money. It may be that the family wants to live in a different area where they think conditions are better. In these cases the family chooses to move because of the attractions of the new place and because they have the means and freedom to do so.

Many families live in rented flats or houses. They may have to leave if the rents are raised so high that they cannot pay them, or if a member of the family becomes unemployed and is unable to earn a wage. On other occasions older houses or flats may be demolished to make way for new developments, and people then have to be rehoused elsewhere in the town or even further away. A family may move from choice because they raised enough money to buy a house of their own.

There are other reasons for moving. If a person's factory, shop or office closes down or is moved to another place then he or she will have to find another job. If there are no jobs in the area then that person may have to move with his family to wherever there is work.

Many people move home when they retire. A lot of older people look forward to the chance to be able to move to a home by the sea or in the countryside, when they no longer have to go to work. Other old people choose to move to a house or flat in the same neighbourhood. Later on they may move to an old peoples' home where they can be looked after.

For whatever reasons hundreds of thousands of people change their homes, or migrate, within Britain each year.

Moving home

New houses being built on an estate

1 Look at the graph. Why do more people move home between the ages of 20–25 than 30–35? Why do females tend to leave home earlier than males?
2 Describe the sort of place you would like to live in when you move home.
3 What reasons for moving home are described on these pages and on pages 112 and 113?
4 Some people choose to move out from large towns and live in small surrounding towns and commuter villages. They travel into the town each day to work. Why do they choose to do this? How can they manage to do so?

Unemployment and population change in London. What is the link between the two?

Population change % in figures
Unemployment of over 8% in late 70s - the worst six
Unemployment of under 3% in late 70s - the best five

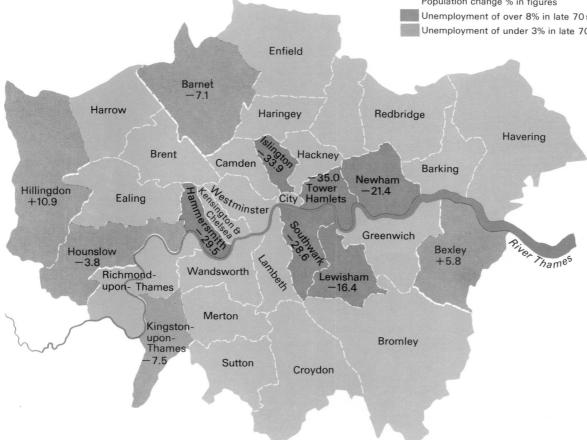

Moving around Britain

Maps and plans

A map of population density in Britain plotted by laser beam. 600 000 coloured dots representing one square kilometre were used to construct this map of Britain's population at the 1971 census. The low population of the hilly areas of the country can be clearly seen. A new pattern will be seen on the 1981 map as populations move.

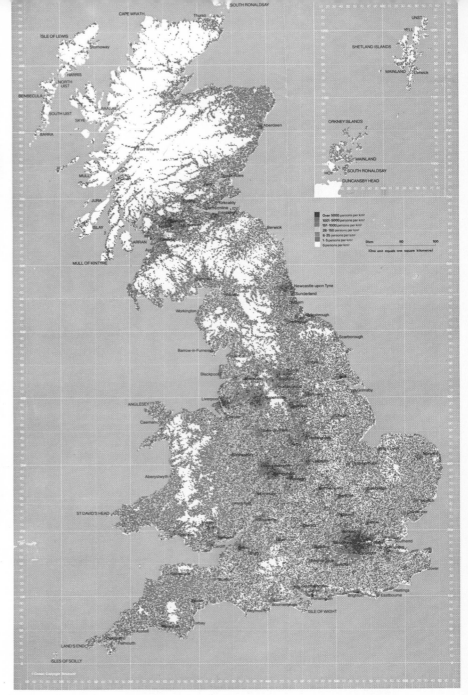

On pages 90–1 you saw some 'memory' or 'mental' maps. These told you what the people who drew them remembered or thought about places. If several people drew memory maps of the same area they would probably look very different. Another kind of map is based on such things as the time or cost of getting from one place to another. Others, like the 'over-ground' map on page 95, show things in the correct order but not in the correct place.

'True' or accurately drawn maps are quite unlike these. They should not vary from person to person since they are based on careful measurements. The most usual maps are true-to-scale. They show things in the same positions as they appear in real life on the ground.

True-to-scale maps also differ. One big difference is their scale. On page 91 the map shows streets and individual houses. This is known as a large-scale map or a 'plan'. The Ordnance Survey Map of

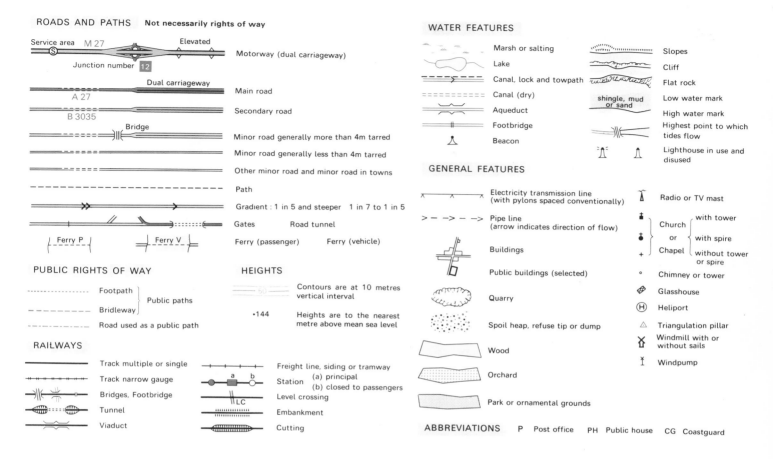

ROADS AND PATHS   Not necessarily rights of way

Motorway (dual carriageway) — Service area M 27, Elevated, Junction number 12

Main road — A 27 — Dual carriageway

Secondary road — B 3035

Minor road generally more than 4m tarred — Bridge

Minor road generally less than 4m tarred

Other minor road and minor road in towns

Path

Gradient : 1 in 5 and steeper   1 in 7 to 1 in 5

Gates   Road tunnel

Ferry (passenger)   Ferry (vehicle)

Ferry P   Ferry V

PUBLIC RIGHTS OF WAY

Footpath ┐
          │ Public paths
Bridleway ┘

Road used as a public path

HEIGHTS

Contours are at 10 metres vertical interval — 50

•144   Heights are to the nearest metre above mean sea level

RAILWAYS

Track multiple or single

Track narrow gauge

Bridges, Footbridge

Tunnel

Viaduct

Freight line, siding or tramway

Station   (a) principal   (b) closed to passengers

Level crossing   LC

Embankment

Cutting

WATER FEATURES

Marsh or salting

Lake

Canal, lock and towpath

Canal (dry)

Aqueduct

Footbridge

Beacon

Slopes

Cliff

Flat rock

shingle, mud or sand   Low water mark

High water mark

Highest point to which tides flow

Lighthouse in use and disused

GENERAL FEATURES

Electricity transmission line (with pylons spaced conventionally)

Pipe line (arrow indicates direction of flow)

Buildings

Public buildings (selected)

Quarry

Spoil heap, refuse tip or dump

Wood

Orchard

Park or ornamental grounds

Radio or TV mast

Church or Chapel   with tower / with spire / without tower or spire

Chimney or tower

Glasshouse

Heliport (H)

Triangulation pillar

Windmill with or without sails

Windpump

ABBREVIATIONS   P   Post office   PH   Public house   CG   Coastguard

Southampton shows all the streets and roads, but not individual buildings. The map of the Lake District shows only the outline of the towns and only the main roads. By comparison with the street map this would be called a small scale map. Finally the map of Britain on this page shows even less detail. As the scale of the map changes so the detail gets less but the area of land shown gets greater. All the maps are correct, but they are not all suitable for the same purpose. You could not find your way around Southampton from the map of Britain, and you couldn't tell where other towns in Britain were from the map of Southampton!

Not only do the scales of maps differ. They often show different things. Some of the maps of Britain show mountains and caves, others show steelworks and power stations. We need a key to tell us what the symbols on the map stand for. The list of symbols are given in a key. Without a scale and a key a map is not very useful.

1   What is the distance represented by 10 centimetres on the maps on pages 39, 61, 62 and 111? Write the answers in the following way. 'On the map of..... on page...... 10 centimetres represents ......'

2   Which of the maps and which of the scales shows lots of detail? Which of the maps and which of the scales shows most land?

3   On the Southampton map give the symbol (if there is one) and Grid Reference of a park or ornamental ground; a parking site; a bus or coach station; a flare at the oil refinery; the Civic Centre; the Ocean Terminal and a beacon.

This key shows some of the symbols used on the Ordnance Survey 1:50 000 map

How to use or give Grid References

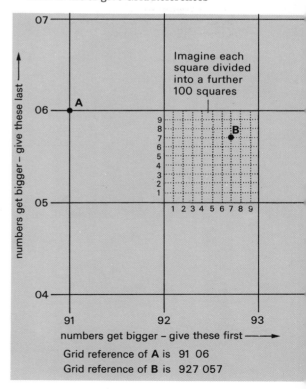

numbers get bigger – give these last

Imagine each square divided into a further 100 squares

numbers get bigger – give these first →

Grid reference of **A** is 91 06

Grid reference of **B** is 927 057

Passenger travel

Cross Channel ferry and hovercraft

Main air and sea passenger ports

A lot of people travel from Britain to other countries. They may do this as part of their work, for a holiday, to see friends or to emigrate. Large numbers of people also travel into Britain for similar reasons.

Because Britain is an island these journeys must be made by air or sea. Before the days of air travel, of course, they all had to be made by sea. If the Channel Tunnel is built there will be a third way of getting in and out of the country.

In the past great passenger liners used to start and end their long ocean voyages at most of Britain's bigger ports. Nowadays the only important long-distance passenger port is Southampton, although some passenger ships use Tilbury which is the part of London docks nearest the sea.

There has been a very big increase in recent years in shorter sea journeys across the Irish Sea, The North Sea and the English Channel. This has been helped by the use of car ferries such as the Sealink service, by Seaspeed and other hovercraft and by the Seajet

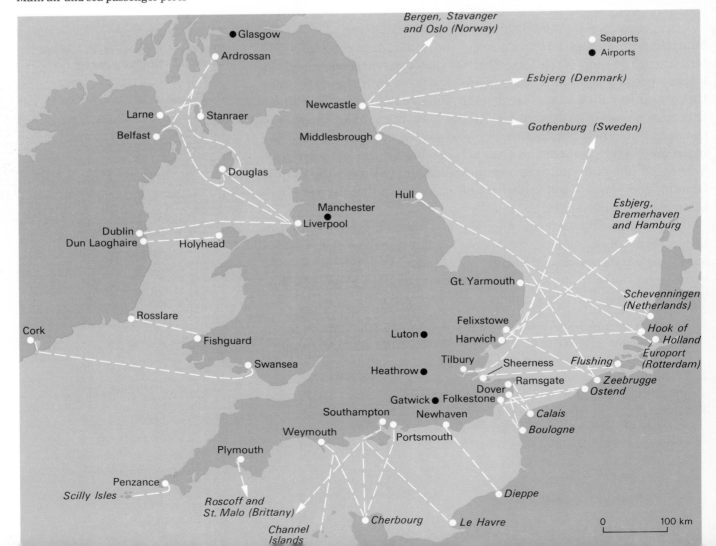

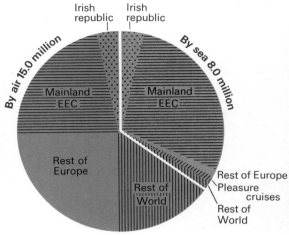

Heathrow airport

Overseas passenger journeys from Britain

A group of fellow-workers setting out on a charter flight from Ringway Airport, Manchester

jetfoil service. Dover handles far more passengers than any other port. It is the nearest port to Europe, and it has the means to handle boat, hovercraft, car ferries and cross-channel rail services.

Heathrow is by far the largest airport in Britain. Most international airlines use it and over 50 000 people work there. In terms of the value (but not the weight) of its cargo it is bigger than any British sea port. But it is still not big enough for future needs. Although there is another rapidly expanding international airport at Gatwick it is likely that London will have a third airport soon. Some airports such as Luton are best known as places from which charter flights take people on holiday to Spain and elsewhere in Europe, while others handle mainly air traffic within Britain.

Sea and air ports need special buildings and equipment to handle the ships and aeroplanes. Airports also need huge areas of land for the runways used by Jumbo jets and planes like Concorde.

1 Why have air journeys replaced longer ocean sea journeys but not shorter journeys by ferry?
2 The four leading airports are Heathrow, Gatwick, Manchester Ringway and Glasgow. What do you notice about their location? Why must airports be located on the outskirts of towns? Why is this annoying to airline passengers? Why are so many people objecting to the building of a third London airport?
3 Name your nearest airport and seaport. Say why you would like to take a journey in either Concorde or on a Seaspeed hovercraft.
4 Look at the graph. Do most people go abroad by air or sea? To which area do most people from Britain go a) by sea, b) by air. Try to explain the difference.

Seaport

Southampton is one of Britain's biggest ports. It can handle ocean liners, general cargo ships, container vessels and oil tankers. It also has docks where hovercraft and hydrofoils can take passengers on and off.

There are several reasons why Southampton has become such a big port. The piece of land jutting out into Southampton water between the Rivers Test and Itchen gives a lot of water frontage for docks. Because there are two tides a day and a deep channel in Southampton Water large ships can get right into the docks. The tidal range (the difference in level of water between high and low tides) is low so lock gates are not needed at the docks. The north-west to south-east direction of the channel means it is protected from south-westerly winds. Finally, Southampton is well-placed for links with France and for ocean traffic using Atlantic sea routes.

1   Draw a simple map to show the site of the docks and the oil refinery terminal.
2   From the map on page 101 measure the distance from Southampton to Bristol, Birmingham and London. Describe the location of the port.
3   The container port is the white area around Grid Reference 385123. Give the Grid References of the Ocean Terminal, ferry hydrofoil terminal, vehicle ferry terminal and the centre of the oil tanker terminal.
4   Can you see signs of waterside industries on the map?

Southampton docks. The Ocean Terminal is in the centre of the picture. Try to find it on the map opposite

Fawley refinery and tanker terminal. It should be easy to find the refinery on the map opposite. Why?

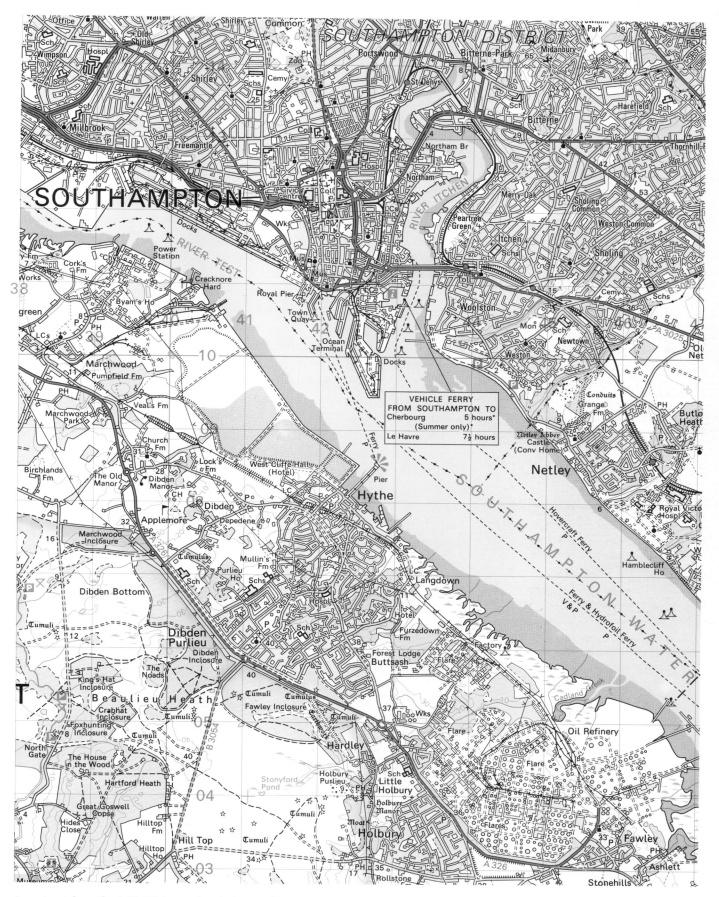

An extract from the 1:50 000 (second series) map of Southampton (refer to key on p107)

To and from Britain

A migrant family leaving for Australia

Right, below: A Russian political refugee waves to well wishers on his arrival in Britain

Net migration into and out of the British Isles in 1977

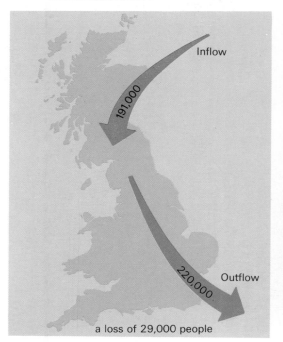

Inflow

191,000

Outflow

220,000

a loss of 29,000 people

A lot of people move into and out of Britain each year. Those moving into the country are known as immigrants and those who move out as emigrants. This has always happened. In our early history wave after wave of invaders came to Britain from the mainland of Europe – Romans, Anglo-Saxons, Danes, Jutes and finally Normans. More recently many Irish have made their home in Britain, while other aliens (people from a different country) settled in this country as a result of the Second World War.

Britain was once a very powerful nation with a big army and navy. People from Britain traded with, lived in and sometimes conquered large parts of the world. Those areas ruled from this country became part of a huge British Empire. Some of these places such as Australia, New Zealand and North America had only small populations of Aborigines, Maoris, Red Indians and Eskimos when the Europeans arrived. Others such as India and West Africa had a big and varied population.

One by one the countries of the British Empire gained their independence. Some, like the U.S.A., Ireland and Burma left it for good, but most joined together to form what is known as the Commonwealth. The countries to gain their independence later are known as New Commonwealth countries. They include India, Sri Lanka, Bangladesh and the countries of the West Indies, Nigeria and the other Africa states. Pakistan is one country that has now left the Commonwealth.

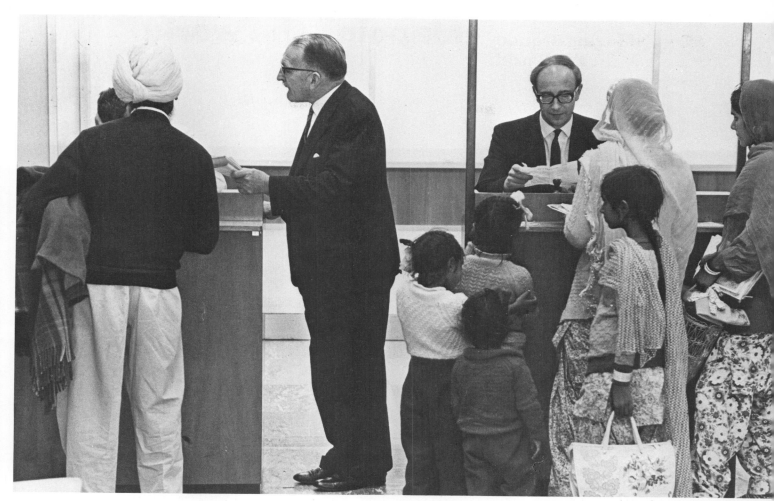

From the mid 1950s onwards large numbers of people from the New Commonwealth migrated to Britain. This was mainly because the opportunity for work was better than in their own countries, and Britain needed workers in certain jobs. In 1973, largely because of concern that great numbers of people of different backgrounds concentrated in some of the larger cities of Britain would cause tension, a limit was set on the number of immigrants allowed each year.

People migrate into and out of Britain as they have always done. If we put the numbers of migrants together we get a 'net' gain or loss through migration.

1 What was the net migration for Britain in 1977? Did more people migrate into or out of the country?
2 There are many reasons why a person or a family might want to migrate. Give one sad and one happy reason for migrating.
3 Draw a bar graph to show the net migration in Britain resulting from the following net movements; **a**) Aliens: + 15 000, **b**) Old Commonwealth: + 3 000, **c**) New Commonwealth: + 20 000, **d**) United Kingdom: − 67 000. Now do the sum 15 000 + 3 000 + 20 000 − 67 000 = ...
4 Name the countries from which any aliens you know come. In which continents are these countries? Are the aliens visitors or have they migrated to this country?

Immigrants going through a customs check (*above*). Meanwhile a little girl waits for her parents to complete the formalities (*below*)

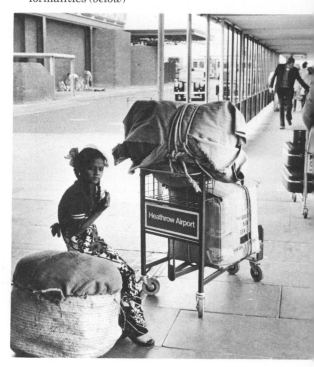

Mapping the world

A photograph of the earth taken from space

Right, above: A globe shows the shapes of the continents more accurately than a map. Why?

For many thousands of years men thought that the earth was a flat surface, and that if anyone went far enough in any direction he or she would fall off the edge! Then a number of thinkers and travellers began to claim that the world was round. This was first worked out by brilliant scientists from observations of the stars and planets, but it was not until 1522 that the first ship completed a voyage all the way around the world. Since then hundreds of thousands of such voyages must have been made, and it is now common for aircraft to make rapid round-the-world flights. In recent years many satellites have been put into orbit round the earth and these send back detailed pictures of the earth from space. Such photographs are another proof that the earth is round. They are also proof that the shapes of the continents on the map are correct. Some satellite photographs are so clear that they are just like looking at a map.

It is not easy to draw a map of a round object like the earth on a flat piece of paper! Any map of the world – other than a globe – is bound to be wrong and distorted in some way or other. All sorts of ways are used to try and make maps of the world make sense, but you need to be very clear about the different methods. Most globes have two sets of

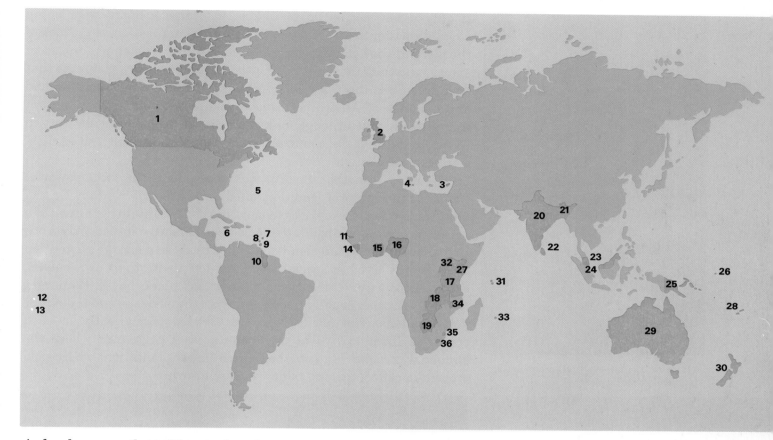

1 Canada 23 million	10 Guyana 830,000	19 Botswana 675,000	28 Fiji 559,000
2 Britain 56 million	11 The Gambia 495,000	20 India 604 million	29 Australia 14 million
3 Cyprus 560,000	12 Western Samoa 151,000	21 Bangladesh 71 million	30 New Zealand 3 million
4 Malta 300,000	13 Tonga 90,000	22 Sri Lanka 14 million	31 Seychelles 60,000
5 Bermuda 218,000	14 Sierra Leone 3 million	23 Malaysia 12 million	32 Uganda 11 million
6 Jamaica 2 million	15 Ghana 9 million	24 Singapore 2.2 million	33 Mauritius 881,000
7 Barbados 254,000	16 Nigeria 79 million	25 Papua/New Guinea 2.8 million	34 Malawi 5 million
8 Granada 110,000	17 Tanzania 14.5 million	26 Nauru 7,500	35 Swaziland 530,000
9 Trinidad and Tobago 1.1 million	18 Zambia 4.5 million	27 Kenya 12 million	36 Lesotho 1 million

A map of the world showing the Commonwealth countries. The shapes are badly wrong in two areas. Can you guess why?

circles drawn on them. Those going through the north and south poles are called lines of longitude. They are all the same size. Those going around the world at right angles to these are called lines of latitude. These include the equator and the Tropics of Cancer and Capricorn. You will notice they get smaller and smaller near the poles. In drawing maps these lines of latitude and longitude are drawn first and then the shapes of the continents are added. Shading, symbols and a key are then added to tell us what the map or globe shows.

1   Compare the photograph of the earth from space and the globe. What is one advantage and one disadvantage of each for telling us what the world is like?

2   Using your atlas, answer the following questions; **a**) what line of longitude passes through London **b**) what is the latitude of the Equator **c**) what is the latitude of the south-west tip of Britain?

3   In the map of countries of the world, what is wrong about the size and shapes of the areas near the north and south poles? Look carefully at any world maps that appear on TV. Try to see how accurate they are.

4   Use the key of the world map to explain what all the countries shaded in red have in common.

Britons abroad

A familiar British-style pillar box in the middle of Hong Kong

If only a few people go to live in a foreign country with a big population they are unlikely to make a great impression on the look of the place. If they go in larger numbers to settle in an empty or almost empty land then they will build cities, farms, railways and ports that look much like those in their homeland. Although much of the land and climates of Australia, Canada and New Zealand are different from Britain, and although many non-British people have now settled there, parts of these countries show many signs that the earliest settlers were British.

We have seen that Britain was once one of the most powerful countries in the world, and controlled large areas of it. Many British families lived in these places. Some returned to Britain at the end of a period of service, while others settled permanently abroad. When the British went to foreign countries that already had a large population they usually lived in special parts of a town with their own houses, shops, schools and clubs. Some mixing took place, but in the larger towns the British usually lived apart from the Africans and Indians or West Indians. The few British that settled permanently in such countries liked to live in the mountains or highlands where the climate was cooler. Many of them ran farms or plantations where cash crops like coffee, tea and bananas were grown.

Indian railways are an important reminder of British rule of India. A clue about the past can often be found in signs and the written and spoken language, as in the Indian Railways safety regulations (*above*). The steam locomotive still in use (*right*) was probably built in Britain

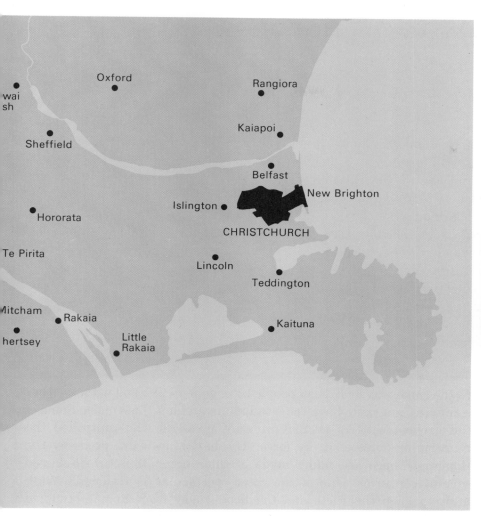

Left: This map of the area around Christchurch in New Zealand shows how the British took the names of their towns to the other side of the world.

The style of this West Indian church is similar to that of many English churches

The centre of Nairobi looks very much like that of many British, European and American cities

When the British ruled a country they usually built roads, railways, irrigation works, ports and factories as well as creating farms and plantations. They often introduced a British system of education, with Universities which awarded English degrees. Their legal system often followed the English model (including wigs!) and their Civil Service was run along British lines. Even though most of these countries are now independent there are still many things to be seen that remind us that British people once lived and worked there. The most important of these, of course, is the English language, which has become the official language of many of these countries.

1   From your atlas find out in which continents are India, New Zealand, Canada, Nigeria and Jamaica.
2   Look at the map of a part of the South Island of New Zealand. Which names are of British origin? Where are the British towns that gave their names to these on the other side of the world?
3   Who were the inhabitants of **a**) Australia, **b**) New Zealand, **c**) Canada and **d**) South Africa that were overrun, often by force, by early British settlers?
4   Using your atlas locate the towns in Britain which lent their names to the settlements in New Zealand shown on the map above.

Migrants to Britain

Right: Hadrian's Wall, built by the Romans

The Mosque in Regents Park. Mosques are the 'churches' of the Moslem religion

In the same way as British people have gone to live and work in other countries, migrants have come to Britain and left their mark. Some of the earliest settlers in Britain were invaders who controlled the country, or parts of it, by force. The best known are probably the Romans. There are many signs of their occupation, which lasted several centuries. One of the most spectacular is Hadrian's Wall, built to keep the Picts and the Scots away from Roman-occupied Britain.

Some parts of our cities have always been places where immigrants have concentrated. In London one of the best known of these places is Soho with its Italian, Greek, Spanish, Hungarian and other European shops and restaurants. In ports such as Liverpool or Cardiff there are 'quarters' where Indian and Chinese seamen and their families live. Some cities including Liverpool and Glasgow have large Irish areas.

When we talk of immigrants to Britain nowadays, though, we usually think of migrants from India, Pakistan, Bangladesh, East Africa or the West Indies. This is not so much because their numbers are very great, but because their colour, language, religion and way of life is different from that of people who have lived in Britain for many generations.

Because migrants want to be near people like themselves, often from the same towns and villages, they tend to concentrate in just a few places. They feel more at home with the same language and customs and often find that houses and jobs are easier to get in these areas. Only slowly do the different groups begin to follow other habits and customs. When migrants concentrate in one area, whether it is the British in Calcutta or Indians in London, they tend to make a strong impression on the place.

An advertisement for an Indian film in Southall

1 From your atlas find out in which counties are **a**) the part of Hadrian's Wall near Newcastle, **b**) Regents Park, **c**) Cardiff, **d**) Southall.

2 Read the extract about Southall. What is the link between the Punjab and Britain that encouraged Punjabis to come to Britain? What reasons are given for the concentration of Indians in Southall? Read the first sentence again – what jobs were available in the 1950s?

3 What are some of the disadvantages of immigrants and their families concentrating in one place? Even if immigrants wanted to spread out through the city, why is it sometimes difficult for them?

4 What are some of the visible signs (other than the people themselves) that **a**) Irish, **b**) Italians, **c**) Indians, **d**) Pakistanis, **e**) West Indians live in an area? Choose one or two of these immigrant groups.

A newspaper article about the Indians in Southall

Southall Immigrants form a tightly knit community

A tributary of the Sutlej flows through Southall in the shabby industrial suburbs of western London. It has one of the highest concentrations of immigrants in the United Kingdom... At present the best guess available is that Southall has a population of about 70 000 of whom between 20 000 and 30 000 are immigrants or children of recent immigrants. Most of the immigrants are Indians, most of them Sikhs from the northern Punjab... Over the past 20 years a fair-sized town has been transported half across the world from the Punjab to Southall. Its inhabitants are bound together by family ties, language, custom, local patriotism and a feeling of being visitors in a strange and perhaps hostile land...

Within memory Southall has changed from a small, neat and clean village in the country into a foreign town. But it is a town with energy and hope. After the present summer storm, the two cultures will get back to learning to live side by side.

People of Asian and West Indian origin shopping on an English High Street

119

The spread of ideas and information

Kenneth Kaunda, Prime Minister of Zambia, and Margaret Thatcher, British Prime Minister, at a conference of Commonwealth Leaders

Right: How information spreads – by word of mouth!

The importance of the printed word in our daily lives: paper-making and printing was invented in ancient China

It is easy to see how people and goods move from place to place. Information, ideas, ways of doing things and customs can also spread from one area to another.

When transport was slow and difficult very few people travelled between different parts of the world. Our word for European people who travelled in distant lands is 'explorer', although this word covers people who travelled for different reasons whether to trade, settle, fight or spread religion. We must not forget that at the same time Arabs, Chinese and other non-European travellers were 'exploring' our countries. Wherever such people went, their language, clothes, weapons, religion, tools and ways of doing things were strange and difficult to understand to those they visited. The travellers took back stories of these strange places to their own countries.

As time went on many of these different groups got used to each others language and behaviour. They understood each others beliefs

A ● tells ■ tells ▲ tells ● tells □ tells △ tells ○
(5 mins) (10 mins) (15 mins) (20 mins) (25 mins) (30 mins)

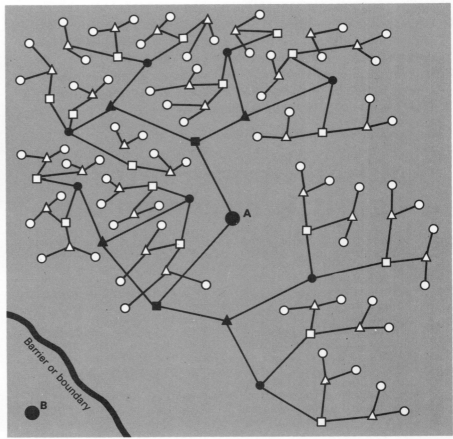

Left: British agricultural expert helping farmers in the tropics. Chipembe Farm, Tanzania

A poster in an African country for a familiar British drink

and ways of doing things. If a country had been conquered, it probably had to obey the laws and follow some of the customs of the invading army. Either through choice or force, ideas and customs from one area slowly spread into others through this sort of direct contact.

By this method it took a very long time for information, ideas or inventions to spread or 'diffuse' throughout the world. With the discovery and world-wide use of the telephone, radio and television, and with the ease and speed of travel these days, it has become much quicker. Events on the other side of the world can be seen as they happen. Experts or students of all sorts can travel around the world to explain new ways of doing things or to study. Some companies, known as multi-nationals, have offices in many different parts of the world. Information can be stored and passed by books, micro-film, videotape and computer.

Many of the things we do or use in Britain were first thought of or developed elsewhere, while many of the ideas and inventions and customs that started in Britain are now found throughout the world. The greatest change nowadays is the speed with which the spread of information and ideas is taking place.

1 Look at the diagram. If a man or woman gets a piece of news or an idea and tells two people within five minutes, and they both tell two more people within five and so on, how many people will know after thirty minutes?
2 If all the people in the diagram were listening to the person at A broadcasting a piece of news on the radio or television, how long would it take for them all to hear it? Name one advantage and one disadvantage of this method of spreading news.
3 What are some of the 'barriers' that might stop people in area B from hearing information that spreads from area A?
4 Do you always change your habits when you hear of different ones? Do you believe all the information you receive? If not, why not?

Red Adair: an American expert on oil blow-outs arrives in Britain. His special skills are in demand all over the world

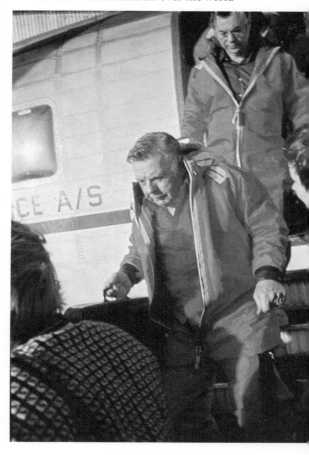

Sport and entertainment

Cricket is played throughout the West Indies in all sorts of conditions

Right: Bjorn Borg: a Swedish tennis star

East meets West in a Judo contest

When you watch an international tournament like World Cup football, it is hard to believe that not so long ago it was a game that was unknown outside our own country. The same applies to many other sports such as Tennis, Golf and Cricket.

It is interesting to find out how, when and where certain games started and how they then began to be played in other countries. Football and cricket have spread from England in very different ways. Football is nowadays played in almost every country in the world. Cricket has not spread or diffused so widely. Almost all the countries that play the game were once part of the British Empire. The soldiers, civil servants, traders and settlers that lived in these distant lands played cricket there and it was adopted by the local people. Now that they have gained their independence they still play the game that originated in England.

Another example of the spread of ideas and customs is in the world of entertainment. Both 'classical' and 'pop' music is played throughout the world. Entertainers give live concerts on tours all over the world. Recordings made in one country can be seen or heard in millions of homes in other countries throughout the world on record, cassette and tape players as well as on TV and radio and in the cinema.

Carnival at Notting Hill, London

Some entertainment associated with a particular part of the world has spread to other places. A good illustration of this is the annual Carnival in Notting Hill in London. The home of Carnival is South America and the West Indies – it varies from island to island. West Indians or their descendents living in London are continuing the tradition thousands of kilometres away from where it began.

Music, dance, sports, customs and ideas all move from place to place as do people, goods and machinery.

Elton John sightseeing in Moscow, while on a tour of Russia

1 The World Cup semi-finalists in 1978 were Argentina, Holland, Italy and Brazil. Which continents are these countries in?
2 Which of the following Commonwealth countries or groups of countries play Test cricket and which do not? England (a part of the United Kingdom); Canada; Australia; Nigeria; India; Malawi.
3 Where are the following sports and entertainments followed by very many people; Judo, bull-fighting, baseball, ice-hockey, hurling, yoga? Have they spread to Britain? If not, how have you heard of them – if you have!
4 Name two American TV programmes that you watch regularly. Name any TV programme that you have seen recently that told you something about life in another country. Was it a documentary or a story? Was it fact or fiction?

Communications in the future

It is hard to realise that when our grandparents were children there were few cars or aeroplanes, and no television sets. Change has been very great and very fast, and it seems to be speeding up all the time. It is impossible to be certain what travel will be like in twenty years' time, but there are a few clues.

The Advanced Passenger Train will be coming into service in the early 1980s, and this will mean that passenger travel between our cities will be very fast and comfortable. These trains were designed for speeds of up to 250 km per hour, and could reduce the time of the journey from London to Newcastle from four hours to just over two hours.

In the late 1970s it became clear that there was always going to be a shortage of oil, and that if care was not taken it would all be used up. Cars, lorries and buses are great users of petrol, and a lot of research has gone into trying to develop an electric car. Although they exist they are not a practical possibility for general use at the moment. But electric cars for most people could well be a possibility by the year 2 000 bearing in mind the inventions and developments of the past twenty years.

The Advanced Passenger Train

The Space Shuttle, now being developed in the United States. It is planned to be used again and again and will replace the rocket as a means of taking men into space

Japan

CHARGE BAND 5B · Time difference 9 hours later than GMT

International Code 010	Country Code 81	Area Code	Subscriber's Number

Amagasaki	6	Kobe	78	Sakai	722
Chiba	472	Kyoto	75	Sapporo	11
Fukuoka	92	Nagasaki	958	Sendai	222
Hamamatsu	534	Nagoya	52	Shizuoka	542
Hiroshima	822	Okayama	862	Tokyo	3
Kawasaki	44	Osaka	6	Yokohama	45

Kenya

CHARGE BAND 5A · Time difference 3 hours later than GMT

International Code 010	Country Code 254	Area Code	Subscriber's Number

Mombasa	11	Nairobi	2	Nakuru	37

Tones similar to those used in the U.K.

Part of a page from the International Telephone Guide

Space travel may have seemed more like science fiction twenty years ago. Since then astronauts and cosmonauts have shown it is possible, and men have walked on the moon. It is very likely that there will one day be satellite space stations where men and women will spend long periods of time servicing space travel and doing scientific work of one sort or another.

In 1979 the Post Office opened its new satellite communications station at Madely near Hereford. It receives and transmits signals through a satellite 3 600 kilometres above the Indian Ocean. There were over 200 such satellites in the world in the late 1970s, and many more are planned. Millions of phone calls, broadcasts and masses of computer information is passed by these stations. The first Madely aerial carried 2 000 phone calls at any moment, and about a million a month between Britain and forty other countries. With these and other developments in communications like the Prestel system it will be possible to contact people, obtain information and speak to people all over the world within seconds.

This telecommunications advertisement is entitled 'No need to go to the office'. This man is sitting at his 'home unit' which provides, by electronic means, all he needs to do his job

1   Try to find out from books or your grandparents what travel was like about 50 years ago. What were the main methods of transport? How far did most ordinary people travel each day or on holiday? How long did it take to cross the Atlantic or go to Australia?
2   Think of some of the disadvantages of rapid travel. In many ways although long distance travel is getting quicker, short term travel is slowing down. How do you explain this?
3   What number would you dial to talk to someone at the telephone number Tokyo 3421? (It would have cost £1.21 for one minute in 1980). How many hours' difference in time is there between Britain and Japan? Japan is ahead of Britain, so if you phoned at mid-day from Britain, what time would it be in Tokyo?
4   What are your feelings about space travel or about immediate communications with people all over the world – do you think it desirable or undesirable?

Britain in the future

An example of modern British office building. Houses opposite are reflected in its glass walls

A population pyramid. Britain in the mid-1970s

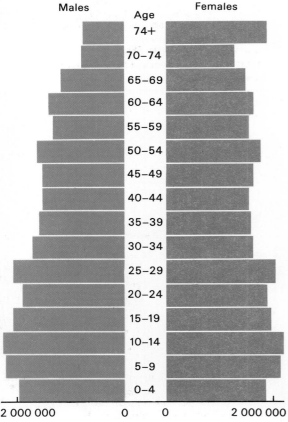

All we can say with any certainty about the future of any place is that it will be different. Some mines and factories will be closed down while others will be started in what is now countryside. Some parts of towns will decline, others grow. The pattern of the landscape will be different. Because of the speed of change it is likely to be very different in Britain in the year 2000 from what it is now.

A lot will depend on how many people there will be. This will depend partly on how many babies are born and how many people die each year. If there are more births than deaths, then the population will grow, unless there are enough emigrants to wipe out the difference. The size of families changes quite a lot, and nobody can be sure what the average family size will be. What does seem likely is that people will live to a greater age, and so there will be a large number of people who have retired from work. This is unlike many countries where the proportion of very young people in the population is very high.

Another feature of the population is that there will be a fair number of people from other Commonwealth and foreign countries. A lot of the immigrants are black and their sons and daughters are black British. The total of black people in Britain is not all that high, but they tend to concentrate in particular areas where they may form a large part of the population. Some people are worried by the different religions, colour and customs of these immigrants and their families while others feel that they add a great deal to our way of life. Britons of the future will be living and working in a multi-cultural country.

Work in the future: an automated factory in Italy made these cars for use in Britain

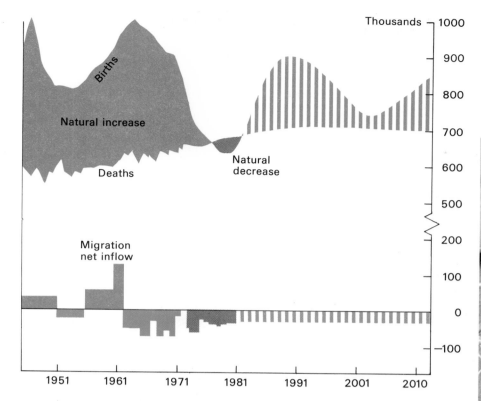

Thousands

Births

Natural increase

Deaths

Natural decrease

Migration net inflow

| 1951 | 1961 | 1971 | 1981 | 1991 | 2001 | 2010 |

Left: Natural change and net migration in Britain between 1945 and 2000 (actual and estimated)

Britain in the future will be a multi-cultural society

Member countries of the EEC
Countries that have applied for EEC membership
Other countries

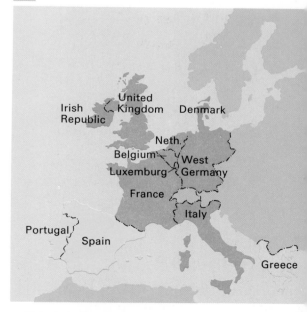

Britain in Europe. The countries of the European Economic Community

We have seen some of the ways in which town and countryside are changing, and how people work and travel to work. Many people believe that a revolution is about to take place in work. As more and more work is done by computers and automation, there will be fewer jobs for people. Everyone will have to work less, or some people will never have a proper job. We shall all have more non-working time. There may well be less need to live in big towns and cities. Communications may improve. This could be another factor which will decide where we live.

Britain is no longer the powerful country she once was, but still has many links with the rest of the world, lots of wealth and skill and can play an important part in the world in partnership with other countries. That is one reason why the next twenty years are likely to see much closer links with neighbouring countries in Europe.

1 When did the natural increase of population change to a natural decrease? If the projection (which is a careful guess!) is correct, when will there start to be a natural increase?
2 What are the sorts of reasons why parents have large families? Why do they sometimes have small families?
3 How important do you think it is for people to have a job? Would you want a job even if you were given enough money to support yourself and your family if a job was not available?
4 Try and imagine fewer and fewer children being born each year, so that the length of the bars at the bottom of the population graph get shorter and shorter. At the same time the length of the bars at the top will get longer as more people live to a greater age. What will be some of the problems caused by these changes?

127

Acknowledgements

The Publisher would like to thank the following for permission to reproduce photographs:

Aerofilms, pp. 19, 30, 38, 42, 50, 53, 67, 78, 82, 109; Airviews, p. 18; Architectural Association, p. 126; Architectural Press, p. 86; Aspect/Bob Davis, p. 116; Associated Press, p. 112; Steve Benbow, p. 75; Blackpool Council, p. 43; Boving and Company Ltd., p. 16; Bristol City Museum, pp. 56, 57; British Caledonian, p. 98; British Gas, p. 98; British Hovercraft Corporation, p. 108; British Rail, pp. 48, 94, 95, 96, 124; British Steel Corporation, pp. 20, 21; British Sugar Corporation, p. 30; British Tourist Authority, p. 39; British Waterways Board, p. 99; Camera Press, pp. 63, 64, 88; The Civic Trust, p. 85; Bruce Coleman Ltd., pp. 12, 14, 26, 28, 29, 30, 32, 34, 36, 44, 54; Colorsport, p. 122; Crown Copyright, pp. 10, 106; Daily Telegraph Colour Library, pp. 49, 55, 68, 71, 94, 100, 103, 123; Dartmoor National Park Department, p. 93; Patrick Eagar, pp. 102, 110, 122; Esso, p. 110; Robert Estall, pp. 87, 118; Mary Evans Picture Library, pp. 64, 100; Farmer's Weekly, pp. 33, 34; Fiat Motor Company (UK) Ltd., p. 126; Dougie Firth, p. 64; Paul Francis, p. 109; Fay Godwin, pp. 10, 74, 117; Greater London Council, p. 85; Ray Green, pp. 42, 74, 92; Susan Griggs/Julian Calder, p. 75,/Richard Cooke, p. 52,/Anthony Howarth, p. 101,/Adam Woolfitt, pp. 35, 54; The Guardian, pp. 20, 23, 41, 60, 84, 89, 104; Charles Hall, p. 50; John Hillelson/Georg Gerster, p. 52,/Erich Lessing, p. 75,/Fred Mayer, p. 70,/ George Rodger, p. 72,/Brian Seed, p. 88,/Sygma, pp. 120, 121; Hoover Ltd., p. 69; Tony Howarth, pp. 72, 73, 80, 81; Illustrated London News, p. 47; Institute of Geological Sciences, p. 12; ITC, p. 123; Keep Britain Tidy Campaign, p. 87; Keystone, p. 112; London Transport Executive, p. 79; The Mansell Collection, p. 68; Leo Mason, p. 122; Methodist Missionary Society, p. 121; Midland Bank Ltd., p. 38; Milton Keynes Development Corporation, pp. 73, 82, 83; Colin Molyneux, pp. 22, 52, 54, 65, 101, 104; Margaret Murray, p. 121; National Coal Board, pp. 14, 15; Edmund Nuttall Ltd., p. 17; PAAT/ Micro Instruments (Oxford) Ltd., p. 114; Port of London Authority, p. 96; Post Office Telecommunications, p. 125; Press Association, pp. 92, 102; Punch, p. 102; Radio Times, pp. 40, 103; Rowlinson Broughton Ltd., p. 25; Ruston-Bucyrus Ltd., p. 13; South Wales Docks Board, p. 22; Space Frontiers Ltd., pp. 114, 124; Spectrum, pp. 8, 16, 29, 33, 35, 49, 60, 62, 69, 72, 84, 85, 105, 117, 118; Standard Telephones and Cables, p. 125; The Sunday Times, p. 116; Jeffrey Tabberner, pp. 11, 44, 62, 66, 76, 77, 103, 105; Telford Development Corporation, p. 24; The Times, p. 26; Topix, pp. 96, 113, 119, 120; Paul Trevor, p. 68; Ann Usborne, pp. 31, 55; West Air Photography, pp. 8, 10, 12, 27, 36, 40, 46, 57, 58, 93; Reece Winstone, p. 57; Trevor Wood, p. 32; J R Wooldridge, p. 37; John Woolverton, p. 34.

The four map extracts on pages 61, 62, 107 and 111 are reproduced from the 1980 Ordnance Survey 1:2 500 and 1:50 000 Maps with the permission of the Controller of Her Majesty's Stationery Office, Crown Copyright reserved.

The illustrations are by Pavel Kostal/Sunday Times, p. 45; Mark Peppé, p. 58; Richard Smith, p. 26; Tudor Art Agency, p. 9.